What you
What you Say is
What you Get

Best Wishes

Off the Wall

How to Develop World Class Mental Resilience

By John Dabrowski

Published by The Solopreneur Publishing Company Ltd,
West Yorkshire WF9 4PU
www.thesolopreneur.co.uk

The Solopreneur Publishing Company Ltd focuses on the needs of each individual author client. This book has been published through their 'Solopreneur Self-Publishing (SSP)' brand that enables authors to have complete control over their finished book whilst utilising the expert advice and services usually reserved for traditionally published print, in order to produce an attractive, engaging, quality product. Please note, however, that final editorial decisions and approval lies with the author. The publisher takes no responsibility for the accuracy of the content.

ISBN 978-0-9932987-2-1

Printed in the U.K.

Testimonials

'It's a privilege to be the first to review this excellent book. I was lucky enough to attend the official book launch in Nottingham and hear John speak. His energy, passion and authenticity are infectious and I bought the book and read it almost in one sitting – I couldn't put it down. The world we live in is an increasingly challenging one and mental resilience is essential not only to our survival but also our sanity. This is a tremendous book and one everyone should read. Buy it, read it and change the way you think forever along with the results you get in life!'

Simon Gray – Professional Speaker/Trainer/Coach
www.careercodex.co.uk

'Highly Recommended. This book is an easy to read, step-by-step guide, to mental toughness and positivity. Read it all or dip in and out of the chapters as you need, it works brilliantly. If you're running a business or have a lot you want to achieve this book will keep your positivity and energy high, and get you through the tougher times. John is well known as a total expert in his field, with a huge passion for what he does and how he helps people. This book is an inspiration and I use it regularly to keep me on track and focussed.'

Serena Humphrey – CEO F Word Training Ltd
www.fwordtraining.com

'Such a great pick me up - excellent reading to get you back on track. Well worth it for finding the inspiration to make positive changes in your life.'

Maureen Pierre – Air Liquide
www.uk.airliquide.com

'John writes from a wealth of experience in overcoming whatever life throws at you. I found "Off The Wall" enjoyable to read and full of excellent, easy to understand principles along with practical application. This book can change your life for the better. As John says in his first chapter, "what are you waiting for?" Make the decision and get the book, you won't regret it.'

Barry Manson – Church Pastor Charis Church
www.charischurch.org.uk

'Want to change your thoughts from being negative to positive, well read the new book, 'Off the Wall.' I did and now I am approaching my daily activities with more mental resilience. An excellent read that combined theory with practice.'

Ruth Pearson – Motivation Speaker
www.listeningtoyourvoice.co.uk

Acknowledgements

I'd like to take this opportunity to say a special thank you to the following people for all their support over the years. My mother Janina, my brother Richard and his wife Adelle, plus my dear friend Barry and his wife Linda. Also my ex-professional basketball colleague Randy Haefner and his wife Ana Maria. Not forgetting Dave Clarke and his wife Elaine.

A special thank you goes to my sister Christina, without whose help this book wouldn't have been completed on time – she has had a huge input into this project. There is also one person who helped me greatly in my radio sales days and gave me the confidence formula which changed my life – thank you Harry Dunne.

I can't mention everyone who has had a positive influence in my life, but you know who you are and I thank you from the bottom of my heart.

Last, but of course not least, a big thank you to my dear wife Julie, who has come into my life at exactly the right time. She gives me encouragement, hugs and a love that is precious. She provides immense support, allowing me to build a business which is positively impacting many lives.

Contents

Foreword

Why this book? Why me? Well, you have the book in your hand reading this, so why not? Carry on!

John Dabrowski has had an interesting and varied career to date, from professional and international Basketball player to highly successful sales and marketing director. He then moved on to various coaching, training and public speaking engagements via his company JD Mindcoach Ltd. John's personal experiences make his presentation unique and bring it to life. This allows anybody reading or listening to John to not only understand it, but to absorb and take it on-board in a useful context.

And what is 'it'? John has fantastic skills in so many fields, 'it' can be whatever you want to get better at and benefit from. We all need assistance in many things and my personal experience with John was Mental Resilience training for a solo North Atlantic rowing attempt. He was great at setting out the hardships that I would endure and giving me an insight into developing some inner strength techniques to overcome these issues when I would be alone at sea.

John has also been there over the last decade to assist in the many business issues I needed to deal with and he was a great coach and mentor. He provided assistance in my positions as Chief Executive Officer and Managing Director of various national companies. John showed me that sometimes a business or personal issue just needs reframing or reassessing in order to progress. Someone with John's business knowledge, in the capacity of an independent sounding board, will often shed light on a difficult situation and assist in formulating a process to take a solution forward.

Off the Wall details techniques with an appropriate and useful level of information. It often has John's personal experience at the heart of the chapter contents, giving not only a human touch but also a life experience that many of us will relate to. The individual chapters cover all manner of topics in bite-sized pieces, with excellent information to help understand the power of the mind. They include: visualisation, the importance of a positive mindset, relaxation techniques, handling stress and just about everything for our busy lives at home and in the workplace. Each chapter ends with a summary of the main points and an action plan to assist in getting the best from putting into place the methods learnt.

Putting John's experience into this book will be of such value that not only will you want to start reading it immediately, but as soon as it is read it will sit on your bookshelf as an inspiration and 'life tool.' Something to pick up when you need to deal with whatever life throws at you in a personal or business issue.

This won't be John's last book as I know there is so much talent buzzing around in those grey cells. It needs to be capitalised on and recorded so that so many more people can benefit as I have.

Looking forward to book number two already. Well done John.

David Clarke

Introduction

Off the Wall

The smell of the gym hit me as we all marched in and took our positions against the wall – it was a distinct and pungent smell that brought out very negative emotions in me. The PE teacher picked four boys, who he asked to come out and turn around to face the rest of us who were lined up along the wall. This was my first PE lesson in secondary school and I had just turned 12 years of age, and was dreading what was coming next. I had experienced this feeling before when I was in junior school and I knew what was coming.

The boys that the PE teacher had picked were the four captains, who were instructed to each choose a boy from the wall, in turn, to join their team. One at a time, the boys were called out. This was a straightforward process if you were one of the boys picked in the early stages. But as the number of boys reduced, the pressure increased as no-one wanted to be the last boy left on the wall.

As each captain ran his gaze over the boys, I tried to make eye contact and put my hand up pleading to be picked. All this was to no avail and it got down to just a few boys left on the wall, all of whom were in the same boat of not wanting to be the last one picked. I looked along the wall and saw just a few boys left and I hoped that this time it would be different and I wouldn't be the last one. My hopes were dashed when there were just two of us left - and as we waited for what seemed like an eternity, the name of the other boy was called out and I was left on the wall.

This devastated and humiliated me. I felt shame, rejection, and embarrassment; I wanted the floor to open up and swallow me. I slowly walked with shoulders slumped towards the boy who hadn't picked me. It was clear by the look in his eyes and that of the other boys that they just didn't want me in their team. I tried to stay positive but found that impossible. From that moment on, I did all I could to get out of PE. I would be ill, I would forget my kit, or I would play truant – all to avoid the humiliation again.

But luckily for me, that year my mother and father took me to Poland for the first time and I met my uncle, who played basketball for the Polish Army team. He spent time with me showing me how to play basketball. More importantly he told me that I had his DNA and that I had all the potential inside of me to be good at sport. I'm not sure if it was the fact he was almost seven feet tall, or that he was my uncle, but something struck a chord and lit a little fire in my heart. When I got back to England I begged my mum to buy me a basketball, and after a few weeks she did. All I did was to bounce the ball and throw it against a wall.

Things started to change and I started to go to PE again to face the humiliation, but this time I had a belief that I could change things by working hard. Then the day I had dreamed of arrived. I was lined up against the wall and, as usual, there were two of us left. I was resigned to being the last one again but this time, as we waited for the captain to choose, he chose ME! This was both a shock and an extremely emotional moment for me. With my chest out, I walked towards the captain who had chosen me. I saw the look in his eyes that showed that he did want me, and this was amazing – it felt great to finally be Off the Wall!

I looked back at the boy who was left on the wall and vowed that I would never be in that position again. So from that day on I worked hard on my basketball skills and that led to my other sports improving. Then one day, I was one of those captains who picked other boys off the wall. Then I became school captain. Then I progressed to county player, and finally one day I was picked to go to trials for the Under

19 England team. I didn't make it the first year and was cut before the final team was announced. But one year later, just six years after I had been the last off the wall, I was picked for the Under 19 England team. What a remarkable turnaround from being the worst in school to being one of the best in England!

This demonstrated the power of the mind at a very early stage in my life. A brief interaction with my uncle changed everything, and this change was inside my head and nowhere else. My mindset had turned from a disbelieving, negative, energy-sapping attitude to a positive, 'anything is possible' attitude. This had a dramatic effect on my confidence and performance levels, providing a solid foundation for success.

There is one common factor in my transformation from failure to success in sport that is common in all high achievers, and that is hard work. Recent research indicates that all high achievers in sport work harder than those who don't quite make it to the top. This is something I experienced when I was learning to play basketball. I noticed that there were many players with much more natural talent than I had and I was jealous of them, asking myself why I couldn't be blessed with such talent. But as the years went by, these players fell by the wayside one by one. Their work ethic wasn't the same as mine and they expected their natural talent to take them through without the work being put in.

Because I worked harder than they did I slowly caught them up and finally overtook them to make it to full England international and later professional level. Meanwhile, once they started to slide down the rankings, one by one they packed the game up altogether.

I'm here to tell you at the very beginning of this book that there is no 'secret' to making it to the top – it takes hard work. What this book will give you are great techniques to make you accelerate to reach your desired goals, help to develop a positive mindset, and methods to keep you upbeat and energised. Combine these techniques with hard work, and success is much more likely in your chosen field.

Your mind can either make you or break you and spending time getting your mind in a positive state is worth the effort. If you change the inside, you automatically change the outside. By getting your mind in the right place for the vast majority of the day, you will increase your productivity as well as your feelings of well-being.

So let's begin this journey together, where I share the techniques and philosophies that have helped me to discover energy and passion that I didn't know I could have at the age of 61. I have a 19-year plan to be speaking on stage at the age of 80 and I am very excited for the future. I intend to scale the workload down as I get older and travelling around the world is something I love and intend to do plenty of. I have made many mistakes in my life and I will be sharing these and what I learned from them, which will hopefully help you to avoid the same mistakes.

My business is thriving and I am very privileged to help individuals get closer to where they want to be quicker and with less pain. It also helps them develop a positive mindset strategy that they can use for the rest of their lives. I have a passion for speaking to large audiences, training smaller groups and working one-to-one with clients – all of these give me great satisfaction.

In October 2013, I met Julie, whom I married on 9th May 2015. This marriage is something I thought I would never see, as I've previously experienced two failed marriages. However, by going deep inside and getting my mind in the right place, I discovered the type of partner I was really looking for, and more importantly why both the previous marriages failed. I have never experienced such deep affection for someone and we have so much in common we know that this is for life.

Mental Resilience isn't just about being tough and keeping going, it's about a whole raft of areas of your life which should be in balance, including relationships. It is made up of five key pillars that all high achievers possess – these are Commitment, Motivation, Self-Belief, Control and Focus. With these five pillars in place, those people achieve amazing things in life, pushing themselves beyond their perceived limits.

Utilising the power created by developing these five pillars in their lives, peak performers achieve a great deal more – and are often called lucky or well-connected. But the truth is that they make it happen and when the going gets really tough, they are committed to pushing through. They don't give up at the first hurdle; they have great belief in themselves and have developed a positive mindset that drives them on to achieve success.

Success isn't just financial, it's also relational; it's that classic work/life balance ensuring that their relationship with their loved ones is vibrant and happy. The person who has financial success but has lost their marriage along the way is not successful – they are broken. That is why we keep reading stories about the millionaires who seemingly have everything but end up taking drugs, having affairs, or in extreme circumstances committing suicide.

It is important to have balance in your life and that is why developing the five key pillars of Mental Resilience in your life is critical to achieving the things you really want. It is possible to live a fulfilled and happy life, working on something you are passionate about, keeping healthy and maintaining wonderful relationships. This book can show you how.

"We must believe that we are gifted for something and that this thing, at whatever cost, must be attained."

Marie Curie

If you take the actions described in each chapter you will:

1. Benefit from a great Confidence Technique
2. Learn how to stay motivated
3. Sleep better and wake up refreshed
4. Handle stress more effectively
5. Control your emotions better
6. Improve your belief systems
7. Be more mindful and relaxed
8. Increase your energy levels
9. Learn to control your inner voice
10. Be more content through gratefulness
11. Learn to reframe from negative to positive
12. Develop your own Dream Board for success
13. Learn to visualise effectively
14. Have more focus in your life
15. Be even more committed
16. Be calmer and happier
17. Learn a great relaxation technique
18. Develop laser-like focus
19. Learn about your Inner Chimp
20. Benefit from the Law of Attraction

I look forward to sharing this journey with you and I truly hope that you discover some of the amazing truths and techniques contained in these chapters. I believe these really can change your life and move you to the future you desire.

John

Commitment

The capacity of an individual to deal effectively with stressors, pressures and challenges, and perform to the best of their ability

Chapter 1

Commitment – the first key pillar

The capacity of an individual to deal effectively with stressors, pressures and challenges, and perform to the best of their ability

Commitment

The first pillar of Mental Resilience is Commitment. All that are successful in sport, music and business have this in abundance. When they say they are going to do something they do it. Their resolve to achieve what they have set out to do is remarkable and is one of the main reasons they so often make it, alongside the hard work needed for their success.

It doesn't matter which industry we look at, the same common theme occurs – you have to work hard! From Michael Jordan, the best basketball player to ever play the game, to Alan Sugar. Or from Richard Branson to Wolfgang Mozart. It doesn't matter what skills and talent you have – you won't ultimately succeed without putting the hard work in. You may get away with it for a while, but eventually it will start to crumble around you.

Commitment Versus Interest

Why is commitment so important? Because there is a huge difference between being '*interested*' in success and being '*committed*' to it – Interest is merely a dim and distant relation of *commitment.*

Being interested in success is a good start, but that's all it is: nothing more than a start. You can visualise where you want to go, the milestones you want to pass on the way, and you understand some of the things needed to get yourself there.

You're interested in learning how to do some of those things, and you can probably imagine the need to do them. But you will remain exactly where you are if all you are is interested. The resulting behaviour will include:

- Procrastination, or never getting started at all;
- Over-researching, due to the imagined need to have more information;
- Allowing irrelevant distractions;
- Complaining that there is insufficient time for the task;
- Claiming not to have enough money;
- Waiting for the "absolutely right time" to do it.

The underlying emotion that prevents us committing wholeheartedly to our dreams is the fear of possible failure. We doubt our own ability to succeed, our staying power and how qualified others think we are for the task. We also worry about the lack of money, and what everyone else will think if we don't reach our goals.

Conversely, being committed to achieving goals means that you're not only interested in moving forward, you're also fully focused on the outcome, and will do whatever it takes to achieve your desired goal. This is a very powerful distinction because full and unwavering commitment, when properly applied, is an unstoppable force even in the face of apparently insurmountable obstacles.

"Until one is committed, there is hesitancy, the chance to draw back, always ineffectiveness. Concerning all acts of initiative and creation, there is one elementary truth the ignorance of which kills countless ideas and splendid plans: that the moment one definitely commits oneself, then providence moves too. All sorts of things occur to help one that would never otherwise have occurred."

W. M. Murray, 'The British Himalayan Expedition.'

Characteristics of Commitment

Commitment is an action word, so although our commitments start as a thought process, they cannot stay that way. Once a commitment is made we must act on it or the result will be ineffectiveness. Commitment without action is worthless – once we have committed to the right choice, we must act for that choice to have the desired impact.

When you decide to make a commitment to a strategy you have made a positive decision, having painstakingly worked through all the considerations needed to make the right choice. Commitment is the force that drives our choices from concept to reality.

At the heart of commitment is integrity. As you begin to do what you say you'll do, you develop the discipline necessary to succeed. Your integrity and self-esteem grows. Others learn they can count on you. You come to understand the power which enables you to get things done and make things happen.

Similarly, there are consequences when you fail to make commitments or only fulfil those commitments half-heartedly. You fail to get results; your integrity and self-esteem are diminished; others learn they can't count on you. You tend to use excuses to justify not keeping commitments.

"Definiteness of purpose is the starting point of all achievement."

W. Clement Stone

It is important to be honest with yourself and others rather than make excuses. You grow when you accept accountability. It sustains your integrity and allows you to be honest with yourself about what was more important to you than the commitment itself.

It is vital to realise that commitment to success is an absolute – you're either committed or you're not. You can't be 50% committed, or almost committed, any more than you can be partially unique.

Remarkable performance doesn't happen by accident; it is always preceded by commitment. The connection between these two can be described as:

- Commitment is the price you are willing to pay to get remarkable results.
- Performance reveals the price you have paid.

It is important to note at this stage that we all have different personalities and that some people are very happy to retire at 65 years old (or even earlier) and play golf. Others have holidays and enjoy their leisure time whilst some have to keep busy to be happy. All of these and everything in between is absolutely fine; it's what your personality is happiest with that counts.

Clearly I am in the camp of the 'keeping active' brigade, where I need a reason to get up in the morning and have a purpose in life. This gives me energy and makes me happy so my commitment to be working at the age of 80 suits me very well. I don't know if a bus will knock me down tomorrow – I can't control that – but what I can control is my commitment.

Story

When I got a job and moved into the world of radio, I had an attitude of hard work which I took into that position. I worked well and was enthusiastic and I progressed from sales rep to senior sales, and eventually to regional sales manager running a team selling radio across the country.

My work ethic was good and I succeeded because of it.

After 5 years in radio, I decided to leave to try running my own business and things changed for me. Over the next 30 years, I jumped from job to job and my commitment to anything at all seemed to fade away. I would start a new job and do really well in the first year hitting all my targets. Then in the second year I would tell myself that I was really lucky to have this natural talent and that I didn't really need to keep working so hard, so I would take my foot off the pedal.

The following year I would be called into my line manager's office and they would ask me what had happened to me and why my results were not as good as the previous year. I would then try to turn the tap on again and for some reason I couldn't. It was as though I was stuck in second gear and I would work hard for a few days then slack off again. I would then move to another company and start well again, only for the second year to follow the same pattern.

This really frustrated me and I didn't understand what was happening, but now I know that I hadn't truly made a commitment to succeed in that position and because of this it slowly fell apart.

I learned that there are no shortcuts to this. All high achievers have two things in common: commitment and plenty of hard work. I'm sorry to be the bearer of this news but at the ripe old age of 61 I have to agree with this adage. If you want to succeed in anything at all, you need to commit and put the work in.

Now I truly understand the importance of commitment and apply it in my role as MD of JD Mindcoach Ltd. My attitude is completely committed and I am not going to switch off. I understand that smart, hard work is the only way to succeed with my business, together with a good strategy and a positive mindset. Quick recovery from setbacks is essential as is staying healthy and happy.

I have made a commitment to be speaking on stage at 80 years of age. I will, of course, scale the workload down, with a plan to work full-on to the age of 65, then 75% work and 25% play up to 70 years old. Following this it will be 50% work and 50% play to 75, then 25% work and 75% play to the age of 80. I will at that stage review my situation and may indeed carry on.

Because of this commitment I now have an amazing career ahead of me - speaking, training and coaching Mental Resilience and all its components. I have the chance to see the world and do something I am truly passionate about. I dearly love this business where I can help so many people raise their game and unlock that real potential they have but are unaware of. To have found a real passion is a gift and something I am very grateful for.

"Challenges are what make life interesting and overcoming them is what makes life meaningful."

Joshua J. Marine

Summary

- Mental Resilience is made up of five key pillars – Commitment, Motivation, Self-Belief, Control and Focus.
- All high achievers in sport, music and business have commitment in abundance.
- Resolve must be accompanied by hard work to achieve success.
- Being 'interested' in success is very different to being 'committed' to it.
- Commitment can be problematic due to fear, doubt and

worry.

- A truly committed person is an unstoppable force in the face of apparently insurmountable obstacles.
- Commitment is the force that drives our choices from concept to reality.
- Commitment without action is worthless.
- At the heart of commitment are integrity and self-esteem.
- Commitment to success is an absolute – you're either committed or you're not.
- Remarkable performance doesn't happen by accident; it is always preceded by commitment.

Action Plan

1. Correct Your Mindset

Success in any aspect of life starts with your mindset. In order to truly make unprecedented progress, you must make the decision at a core level to hold nothing back. Take a good look at your life and decide that nothing is going to stand in your way – this kind of raw, unrestrained dedication is extremely powerful.

2. Define Your Goals

Vague goals are useless, so before you do anything, get ruthlessly clear about what your ultimate outcome looks like. Decide exactly what you want, how you are going to get there and on what sort of timeline you plan to reach your destination. The key is to define a vision that is so awesome you are willing to do anything to achieve it.

3. Focus on the Important

If you focus on unimportant activities and work hard you still aren't going to get anywhere. Work for the sake of work is not the goal. The goal is to live and work on your own terms, so to achieve freedom you must be ruthlessly selective about what you work on and what you ignore.

4. Make Yourself Accountable
Unfortunately, personal drive may be enough to get you started, but after a week or two your initial enthusiasm slowly begins to fade. So, in order to stay committed, you need a way of holding yourself accountable:

a. Use a Daily Goals system to keep track of your most important tasks – at the beginning of each week, write down your top goals for the next seven days. Then each night before you go to bed, write down two to three of these key tasks that, if accomplished, will leave you satisfied with your day.
b. Tell others what you are doing – at the very least, tell your family about the goals you're trying to reach. Whatever their reactions, getting your ambitions out in the open will help you stay committed.
c. Surround yourself with like-minded people who are rooting for (and expecting) your success. It can provide you with the confidence and motivation you need to take you to a whole new level.

Final Thoughts

If you've been putting off anything in your life, ask yourself why. What are you waiting for? There is something powerful about commitment and determination, which both give you amazing opportunities. There is so much to be said about not giving up on your dream, as the rewards versus the effort involved are huge. You can end up living a fulfilled and happy life where you finish well, so take that step, make that commitment and go for it!

"The achievement of your goal is assured the moment you commit yourself to it."

Mack R Douglas

Motivation

The state or condition of being motivated or having a strong reason to act or accomplish something

Chapter 2

Motivation – the second key pillar

The state or condition of being motivated or having a strong reason to act or accomplish something

Introduction

We all need a reason to accomplish things in life and the bigger the challenge, the bigger the motivation required. In my Mental Resilience Workshops, I often describe motivation this way: ***if the reason you are doing something is bigger than the pain of doing it, you will do it. If the reason isn't bigger than the pain of doing it you will never do it.***

It is easy to make a cup of tea because the pleasure of enjoying the tea far outweighs the pain of putting the kettle on, brewing a tea bag and pouring some milk. However, it's a completely different kettle of fish (excuse the pun) when the bedroom needs decorating, or the garage needs cleaning out and the floor painting, or the tax returns need completing.

Motivation in Practice

The motivation factor comes in to play whenever we have something that needs to be completed or achieved. When I was younger and practising basketball, I needed a reason to shoot the basketball into the basket thousands and thousands of times in order to improve my game. This motivation came with the visualisation of me playing for the England basketball team. I had this vision that I developed using the techniques I have described in the chapter on visualisation. This vision became so strong that it drove me to get up early and stay up late to practise.

I wasn't the most talented player, but I was one of the most motivated, and I simply worked harder than the others and put more hours in. As the months and years went by, I improved at a quicker rate than the other players because of the work I put in and I was the only one from Nottingham who made it into the England team. This was not because I was more talented, but because my motivation level was higher.

On the days when I felt like I just couldn't face another session in the gym, the vision of me in an England tracksuit competing for my country, with the national anthem playing, spurred me on. I have come to realise that nothing worthwhile has ever been achieved without motivation and hard work.

"People often say that motivation doesn't last. Well, neither does bathing. That's why we recommend it daily."

Zig Ziglar

Our job is to find the motivation to get the tough things done. This is easier said than done, but it is possible. I have a Dream Board with 24 things on it – very exciting things that I want to achieve before I die. I visualise having achieved these in great detail every morning, so the images are etched in my mind and have real power. There are times when I feel demotivated to do something that is hard work, but will actually help move my business forward. When this happens I tell myself that if I do this thing in front of me, then it will get me closer to achieving those dreams on my Board.

The detail I go into with each visualisation is the reason they are so real to me. I can feel the heat when I am on the Great Wall of China. I can hear the sound of the helicopter blades as we fly over the Victoria Falls. I can see the children's faces when we visit the orphanage we are supporting. Because these are so real to me, I get things done which I wouldn't otherwise do because achieving these dreams is a big motivation to me

You have to find the right motivation for everything you want to achieve in your business and personal life.

One lady called Granny Brand demonstrates the power of motivation more than anyone I have ever come across, and I want to share her story with you. The details were published in a publication called Word for Today on 7th April 2015 and the title of the true-life story of Granny Brand is 'Do it With all Your Might'.

Story

Evelyn Brand felt called by God to go to India. For a single woman in 1909, a calling like that required a lorry load of faith. She married a young man named Jesse and together they began a ministry to the people of rural India, bringing education and medical supplies and building roads to reduce the isolation of the poor. For seven years, they went without making a single convert to Christianity.

But then a priest in a local tribal region developed a fever and grew deathly ill. No one else would go near him, but Evelyn and Jesse nursed him as he was dying. He said, 'This God, Jesus, must be the true God because only Jesse and Evelyn will care for me in my dying.' The priest gave his children to them to care for after he died – and that became a spiritual turning point in that part of the world. People began to examine the life and teaching of Jesus, and in increasing numbers began to follow him.

Evelyn and Jesse had thirteen years of productive service, then Jesse died. By this time Evelyn was fifty years old, and everyone expected her to return to her home in England. But she wouldn't do it. She was known and loved for miles around as 'Granny Brand', and she stayed another twenty years under the mission board she had served so faithfully. Her son, Paul, came over to see her when she was 70 years old, and this is what he said about his mum; 'this is how to grow old. Allow everything else to fall away, until those around you only see love.'

At aged 70 she received word from her home mission office that they weren't going to give her another five-year term. A party was held to celebrate her time in India, and everyone there cheered her on. 'Have a good trip back home,' they all said. 'I'll tell you a little secret,' she announced, 'I'm not going back home. I'm staying in India.' Evelyn had a little shack built with some resources that she had smuggled in. Then she bought a pony to get around the mountains, and this septuagenarian would ride from village to village on horseback to tell people about Jesus. She did that for five years on her own.

One day, at seventy-five years old, she fell and broke her hip. Her son, Paul Brand, the eminent doctor, said to her, 'Mum you've had a great run. God's used you. It's time to give up now. You can go back home.' She replied, 'I'm not going back home.' She spent another eighteen years travelling from one village to another on horseback. Falls, concussions, sickness and ageing could not stop her.

Finally, when she hit 93 years old, she could not ride a horse anymore. So the men in these villages – because they loved her so much – put her on a stretcher and carried her from one village to another. She lived two more years and gave those years as a gift, carried on a stretcher, to help the poorest of the poor. She died, but she never retired. She just graduated.

This true story of Granny Brand is amazing and hard to believe. As I sit here writing this, I'm in awe of this woman who gave up her entire life to serve the poor, in the most difficult of circumstances. The motivation she needed to continue year after year after year is so huge, but that is exactly how she managed to continue through every setback and disaster. If we can capture this sort of motivation for our lives then we will achieve amazing things.

Whichever way you look at it this is a remarkable story. The motivation she had was bigger than the pain of everything she went through. In her case, it was her faith in Jesus and that motivation drove her to achieve amazing things working right up to her 95th birthday. She believed that this was the reason she was on this earth and no matter what she went through she would continue, otherwise her life would have been a pointless existence.

This level of motivation is extreme, but demonstrates clearly how effective powerful motivation can be. Our job is to discover a big enough reason to take action on everything we are faced with on a daily basis. Whether it is work related or personal, it still requires motivation to begin to take action.

"Fall seven times and stand up eight."

Japanese Proverb

There are many levels of motivation and the higher the motivation, the easier it is to take action and the more we get done. Some famous people have said some very interesting things about motivation.

Story

Andre Agassi is one of the greatest tennis players of all time and one of the few tennis players to hold all four majors in one year. He had great motivation to succeed and his motivation was the fear of loss. In this excerpt from an article, he clearly describes his motivation:

It is 320 yards up the hill Andre Agassi calls "Magic Mountain" on the outskirts of Las Vegas. The desert is on one side; a gated community on the other.

It's Christmas Eve 1999, 38 degrees. Following two hours in the weight room, Agassi sprints up Magic Mountain 14 times. As cars pass by, on the way to holiday dinners, Agassi is sweating, his lungs burning. There's a look of pain in his eyes.

Even Gil Reyes, Agassi's personal trainer since 1990 and the only other person present, wonders what's driving this man.

'I actually stopped him to ask: 'What's making you go?' Reyes said.

'He said, 'Gil, it's just something inside. This is my time. If I don't do it now, I'll regret it so much. That's what it's all about, eh, Gil? No regrets?'

"You just can't beat the person who never gives up."

Babe Ruth

The famous baseball player Babe Ruth demonstrated how the 'never give up attitude' is almost unstoppable. If you're the type of person that never gives up, you're going to be really hard to beat. This goes for competition as well as the universe in general. Sticking with things until you get what you want is the mark of a winner, not just because it shows an indomitable spirit but because it represents a powerful intention. Granny Brand demonstrated this in her life and because of this attitude she helped many thousands of poor people.

Arthur Ashe, the great tennis player, said, ***'Start where you are. Use what you have. Do what you can.'***

This is what Granny Brand did all her life: she just got on with the job in front of her using what she had and gave it her all. It's easy to think that this isn't the right place or the right time, or that you don't have the right resources in order to become a success. You just have to get started right now, from where you are now, with what you have now and your resources will grow as you go along. So don't waste another minute thinking you can't get started on what you really want to do.

The part I love best in the Granny Brand story is contained in the words which follow. *'Her son, Paul, came over to see her when she was 70 years old, and this is what he said about his mum.* ***'This is how to grow old. Allow everything else to fall away, until those around you only see love.'*** This reminds me so much of my mum, who is 92 years old as I write this, and that quote describes her so well.

My mum is a beautiful, loving, caring person who I have never heard say a bad word about anyone and her favourite phrase is: ***'Think happy and you will be happy.'*** She is always laughing, singing and making people happy – wherever she can, she will lift people up and make them feel good.

My wife Julie loves my mum so much – she has never met

anyone so positive and warm. She loves the way my mum encourages her and makes her feel accepted and loved.

My mum's motivation is to make people happy because this makes her happy. What a simple motivation; yet it clearly works for her as this is what she does all the time.

"I've learned that people will forget what you said, people will forget what you did, but people will never forget how you made them feel."

Maya Angelou

Summary

- Motivation is having a strong reason to act or accomplish something.
- Your motivation has to be stronger than the pain of doing what you need to do.
- Motivation gives you the ability to work hard, without which there is no success.
- Find a big enough reason to do something and you will get it done.
- You will hit brick walls along the journey and you need to break through them.
- It's not what happens to you that counts, but how your respond to it.
- When things go wrong, always look for the positives, which are always there.
- When one door closes another one opens – you just need to see the new door.
- How you react to negative things happening to you is a major key to success.
- Make people feel good and they will never forget you.

Action Plan

1. **Visualise in your mind what you want to achieve.** Do this with emotion, using all the senses of taste, touch, sound, vision and smell. Experience the feelings of having achieved what you want to do.
2. **Ignore any negative voices either from people or in your head,** otherwise you will give up before you have completed what you want to achieve
3. **Find the reason this is important to you.** Ask yourself what you will get out of achieving this. Then when you have answered that, ask again to get deeper, and then ask again to get to the real benefit to you. This will likely be one of your core values. Write up the list of reasons in a document you can refer to later.
4. **Write down a list of all your main achievements in life.** This is a powerful tool to help you keep going when things get tough, by reminding you that you are actually good and have had lots of successes in your past. They can be big or small and can be from school, home, social or work areas. For example: passing a driving test, helping someone in need, getting married or starting your own business.
5. **Share your vision with someone positive you trust** and ask them to hold you accountable.
6. **When you hit a difficult obstacle on your way to achieving your goal,** go back to the list of reasons you are doing this to remind yourself and to re-motivate yourself.
7. **Remember that you need to maintain a positive inner voice and positive emotions most of each day,** as you tend to attract what you give out. Work on this, as it is easier said than done. I have found that I am getting better and better at this and, because of that, things are improving in my personal and business life.

Final Thoughts

Motivation is literally the desire to do things. It's the difference between waking up before dawn to go for a run and lazing around the house all day instead. It's the critical element in setting and attaining goals.

Research shows that you can influence your own levels of motivation and self-control, so figure out what you want, grit your teeth through the difficult period, and start being who you want to be.

"What you do today can improve all your tomorrows."

Ralph Marston

Control

Self-control is the ability to control one's emotions, impulses, behaviour and reactions in the face of external demands and is another name for self-discipline

Chapter 3

Control – the third key pillar

Self-control is the ability to control one's emotions, impulses, behaviour and reactions in the face of external demands and is another name for self-discipline

Introduction

Self-control is vital for overcoming fears, obsessions, addictions, or any kind of negative thinking and it puts you in control of your behaviour and your reactions. It helps to develop patience, improve relationships and is an important tool for attaining success and happiness.
Imagine that you are doing something important, like being interviewed for a new job, or preparing for a big meeting. Then suddenly something happens: perhaps an interview question confuses you, or you receive an upsetting call before your meeting. Suddenly you are no longer at your best – now you are nervous, sad, or angry.

If you've ever worried about something, you know how stressed and anxious it can make you feel. It can be hard to let go of the temptation to obsess about a problem, but the thoughts and emotions feed on themselves, becoming stronger and stronger until they overwhelm you.

"Success is the sum of small efforts, repeated day in and day out."

Robert Collier

Similarly, if you've ever had a thought that brought about sadness and you carried on thinking that thought, you know how it can spiral down into depression very quickly. It can be the smallest trigger, but if unchecked the thoughts and emotions can absolutely destroy any good mood you may have been in. Over time this can become so common that it seems normal to feel that way, particularly with people going through divorce or some other loss. They may find that they are crying all the time, unless the emotion is controlled.

If you've ever lost your temper, experienced 'the red mist', or sulked about anything, you know how you felt afterwards. No matter who was at fault, no matter the outcome, you are still left with a very unpleasant feeling because of the outburst. And if you've ever been on the receiving end of a tantrum, it can be quite traumatic.

Losing your temper, sinking into depression and worrying are all negative emotions. They cause stress, they affect your health, and they constantly disturb your sense of well-being and your outlook on life. Self-control is essential in our behaviour to achieve goals and to avoid impulses or emotions that would result in negative outcomes.

Emotions operate on many levels – they have a physical component as well as a psychological one. They operate in every part of a person, affecting many aspects, which is why it is so important to gain control of our emotions and our resulting behaviour. Negative emotions such as fear, anxiety, negativity, frustration and depression cause specific chemical reactions in your body, and studies suggest these can cause chronic illness if not managed properly. Emotions that are not felt, controlled and released, but are buried within the body can contribute to physical illness later.

"I am not a product of my circumstances. I am a product of my decisions."

Stephen Covey

Story

I remember a time when I worked for Metro Radio in the North East of England around 30 years ago and I was fired up. Work was coming in and I was working well. I had been focussing on a large client for over six months and was very close to securing one of the biggest orders in the station's history.

Many hours had been spent on this client and things were looking rosy. I was excited at the prospect of finally landing this client. However, at the last minute the advertising agency I was working with decided to switch the entire budget to TV instead of my radio station. The order that I was just about to secure would have gone a long way to achieving my annual target and I was devastated.

It affected me so badly that for about four days I moped around the radio station fed up with life and hating my job. I came in late, went home early and didn't get much done for that period of time. Then I got another order confirmed and I was back on form again, fired up and raring to go. But I had lost four days!

A couple of years ago I was working on a major client in Wales and it was looking really good for a large contract with my new company JD Mindcoach Ltd. I was excited at the prospect of landing this large contract. At the last minute, they decided not to go ahead and I was down, really down, for... one hour! Then I used a few of the techniques in this book and made a choice to accept it and move on.

I had a good day, a good week and a good month. The four days of negativity I experienced 30 years ago didn't materialise and more importantly it didn't come back and 'get me' later; the negativity simply disappeared with my mindset change. This was very liberating and made me realise that we have a choice as to how we respond to everything we experience. We can choose to go down or get up and dust ourselves off and work out what we have learned from the experience.

"You have power over your mind – not outside events. Realise this, and you will find strength."

Marcus Aurelius

Benefits of Self-Control

- It gives you a sense of mastery over your life.
- It allows you to control your moods and reject negative thoughts and feelings.
- It helps to keep overly-emotional responses in check and brings balance into your life.
- It strengthens self-esteem, confidence and willpower.
- It eliminates the feeling of helplessness and reacting inappropriately to challenging situations.
- It helps to manifest mental and emotional detachment, which contribute to peace of mind.
- It keeps in check self-destructive, addictive, obsessive and compulsive behaviour.

How to Develop Self-Control

So how can we master our emotions under the most difficult circumstances and avoid operating on the wrong types of feelings that spiral out of control? There are basic strategies that can be used in any challenging situation:

- **Don't react immediately.** This can be a huge mistake as it is highly likely that you'll say or do something you'll regret later. Before reacting emotionally, take a deep breath and take a moment to consider what just happened, instead of just instantly reacting to new information or a new situation.

By taking a few seconds to pause and consider, you can calm yourself briefly to produce a better response. Continue to breathe deeply feeling your muscles relax and your heart rate returning to normal as you become calmer.

Do three simple steps to get back on track instantly. When negative emotions strike sometimes you don't have time to work through them until later. To get yourself under control there are three simple things you can do immediately which allow you to accept the emotion without getting caught up in it:

a. The first step is to observe what you're feeling, **name it**, and move on.
   This works because of how the different sections of our brain function. When we are thinking clearly we are using the front of the brain, 'the prefrontal cortex'. Our brain's emotional centre is called the 'amygdala' and this starts taking over when we are getting emotional and cannot think clearly. Naming the emotion brings the prefrontal cortex back into control again.

b. The second step is to **make it normal.**
   Take a moment to realise that what you are feeling for this situation is a normal response. It's nothing earth-shattering or life-destroying. People throughout history have had this emotion, and they've somehow managed to move on despite it. So can you.

c. Once you have named the emotion and normalised it, **laugh at it.**
   If the emotion you are feeling becomes funny or

ridiculous, then it can go away. For example, fear of public speaking causing your legs to shake visibly. If you try to stop this by telling yourself to stop shaking it will only get worse, but if you try to make it worse on purpose it becomes ridiculous, goes away and you are calm.

- **Emotions have a strong tendency to ebb and flow like the tide.** When the impulse you need to control is strong, waiting out this wave is usually enough to keep yourself in control.

  The rule of thumb is to wait at least 10 minutes before succumbing to temptation, after which time you will have things much more in perspective.

- **Focus on what you can control.** Once you have been presented with a stressful situation, try to identify what you can and can't control. If something is done, you can't change it. You can only determine what to do next.

  By focusing on what you can control, you are empowering yourself. By dwelling on things you can't control, you disempower yourself and make yourself more frustrated and more stressed.

- **Decide what is important now.** So many people get very upset about little urgent matters and lose sight of what's really important for them to focus on first. By taking a few moments to pause and consider, you can refocus your mind on what's most important right now and prioritise your plan of action.

  For example, you arrive at an important meeting, get out of your car then realise that you have just left your phone at home. What's important now? The meeting is important now, not your phone. You can deal with the phone situation any time later in the day, so decide that it is not going to upset you.

- **Reframe your thoughts.** Negative emotions tie us to recurring negative thoughts, creating cycles of negative patterns. We need to reframe the situation.

  This skill of turning negative into positive thoughts develops like a muscle and becomes almost instinctive over time. Start by saying "no problem" a lot more - soon you'll condition your mind to believe it.

- **Look at the big picture.** Abstract thinking promotes self-control, so you are more likely to exercise self-control when you don't get bogged down by specific details.

  For example, when working on a long-term project, it's easy to get frustrated by the multitude of small steps required to get you there. Instead, periodically reminding yourself of the end goal helps to prevent discouragement and promote self-control.

- **Know yourself.** Self-awareness is vital and precedes self-control. We must develop 'emotional intelligence' so that we recognise the emotions in which we lack control, such as anger, frustration, sadness, worry, resentment, pleasure or fear.

"Life is what we make it, always has been, always will be."

Grandma Moses

Summary

- Self-control is the ability to control one's emotions, behaviour and reactions in the face of external demands.
- It is vital for overcoming fears, obsessions, addictions, or any kind of negative thinking.
- It puts you in control of your life, your behaviour, and your reactions.
- Emotions need to be controlled – they operate on both a physical as well as a psychological level.
- Self-control strengthens self-esteem, confidence, inner strength and willpower.
- It eliminates the feeling of helplessness and reacting inappropriately to challenging situations.
- It helps to develop patience and tolerance.
- It helps to manifest mental and emotional detachment, giving peace of mind.
- Self-control means not reacting immediately to emotional triggers.
- Emotions tend to ebb and flow in intensity.
- Decide what is most important in any challenging situation.
- Empower yourself by focusing only on what you can control.
- Reframe your negative thoughts into positive ones.
- Look at the bigger picture so as not to get caught up in frustrating details.
- Emotional intelligence will help with self-control once you know yourself better.

Action Plan

1. Prepare in advance

This is a technique to prevent a triggering of the negative emotion. For example, if you know that you're most likely to get angry when you're in a hurry, then don't leave things to the last minute. Get out of the house or office 10 minutes before you need to, and you won't be bothered so much by pedestrians, cars, or slow elevators.

2. Smile

Did you know it's physiologically impossible to have bad feelings if you are smiling? Next time you are feeling sad, or in a rage, just force a smile onto your face. If you wake up feeling bad, just smile at yourself in the mirror first thing in the morning. Just stand there making yourself smile until it's genuine and guess what happens – you will burst out laughing whether you want to or not!

3. Meditate

Buddhist monks appear calm and in control for a reason. Meditation actually trains your brain in self-control (and it improves your emotional intelligence). Techniques such as mindfulness improve your self-awareness and your brain's ability to resist destructive impulses.

Visualise yourself acting with self-control and self-restraint. Take one of the instances where you usually act with a lack of control, and visualise that you are acting calmly and with self-mastery. These are covered in greater depth in Chapter 13.

4. Exercise

Getting your body moving for as little as 10 minutes releases GABA, a neurotransmitter that makes your brain feel soothed and keeps you in control of your impulses.

If you're having trouble resisting the impulse to walk over to the office next door to have a go at someone, just keep on walking. You should have the impulse under control by the time you get back!

5. Eat and sleep well

When attempting to exert self-control your brain uses up your stores of glucose. If your blood sugar is low, you are far more likely to succumb to destructive impulses.

When you are tired, your brain cells' ability to absorb glucose is greatly reduced and your brain's ability to control impulses without glucose is minimal. Also, without enough sleep you are more likely to crave sugary snacks to compensate for low glucose levels. Sugary foods spike your sugar levels quickly and leave you drained and vulnerable shortly afterwards, so eat nutritious whole foods instead.

6. Forgive yourself

In attempts at self-control, a vicious cycle of failing to control oneself followed by feeling intense self-hatred and disgust is common. These emotions typically lead to over-indulging in the offending behaviour.

When you slip up, it is critical that you forgive yourself and move on. Don't ignore how the mistake makes you feel; just don't wallow in it. Instead, shift your attention to what you're going to do to improve yourself in the future.

7. Find a healthy outlet

Emotions should never be bottled up but should be managed and released in a healthy way. Talk to someone you trust or keep a journal and transfer your emotions from your inner self onto the paper.

Final Thoughts

Self-control is vital for overcoming any kind of negative thinking and it puts you in control of your life. Whatever challenges you are facing that may cause stress or negative emotions, you can handle them by exercising control.

In times of stress ask yourself this question: 'Am I going to die right now?' If the answer is 'no,' then realise that you can handle the situation. We know that some situations are extremely difficult to deal with, but step by step, we can find solutions, we can exercise self-control and we can move forward.

"Nothing in life has any meaning except the meaning we give it."

Tony Robbins

Confidence

A feeling of trust in one's abilities, qualities and judgement

Chapter 4

Confidence – the fourth key pillar

A feeling of trust in one's abilities, qualities and judgement

Introduction

The fourth pillar of Mental Resilience is confidence or self-belief. This isn't the show off kind of confidence where 'look at me, aren't I great' oozes out, but it's the quiet inner confidence that allows you to perform really well under pressure.

Your body language, your behaviour, how you speak and how you react to different situations can often portray to others how confident you are and how much belief you have in yourself. Those with confidence are generally more positive about themselves, whereas those lacking confidence often think negatively.

Your level of confidence is not static; it can change and develop. Remember you were born into this world with no sense of what you could or couldn't do. Then, slowly, life started to teach you to limit yourself. A very young child never says: 'I'm not the kind of person who could...' – they haven't yet learned to limit their own horizons or listened to pessimistic people.

Confidence is a great personal resource which enables you to face any situation knowing you can handle it. Without confidence, any situation has the potential to be a threat. Confidence comes from a feeling of self-belief that develops from inside you.

Self-belief is how you think about yourself, the opinion you have of yourself. If you have low self-belief, you tend to have negative thoughts and focus on what you think your weaknesses are. Self-doubts often start to creep in such as:

- 'Can I actually do this?'
- 'Other people are better or smarter than me.'
- 'What will other people think of me?'
- 'Failure is too risky.'

Self-belief is essential: how many things have you not done or tried because you lacked belief in yourself?

Your level of self-belief can be solely due to your own temperament, but negative experiences in childhood can contribute to feelings of low self-belief. People who have been abused or neglected in their childhoods, or who feel they have not lived up to their parents' expectations often have low self-belief. Other things that can also affect it include poor physical health, trauma and social exclusion.

"Nobody can make you feel inferior without your consent."

Eleanor Roosevelt

Story

When I was 18 years of age and in college I remember a particular incident as clearly today as I did all those years ago. This incident happened 42 years ago and every time I think about it all the emotions I experienced at the time come back to me. These emotions were very powerful and had a significantly negative impact on my life from that point on. The incident itself was a very simple affair, where I had to introduce a Professor, who was going to deliver a lecture to four students, all sat around a small table in a small room. On the face of it, this was a very simple thing for me to do, but due to past experiences it became the most terrifying moment of my life to date.

As the hours ticked by towards the moment where all four boys and the professor would be looking at me, my fear grew and I couldn't understand why I was so scared. I remember going to the toilet just before we all sat down in that small room; my palms were sweating, my heart was beating really fast. I had this strange noise in my head that sounded like lots of voices talking at the same time.

We sat down. All four students were looking directly at me and the silence grew longer and longer as I plucked up the courage to utter the first words of introduction. I looked at them, they looked at me and all I could hear were all the voices going off in my head and I froze.

There is no happy ending to this; I simply 'bottled it.' I just wanted to escape out of the room and I turned around to look at the small window behind me. The sun was shining outside and I looked out over the beautiful green grass and wanted the ground to swallow me up. It was a beautiful day but I was devastated, humiliated and embarrassed and I couldn't avoid the whole thing. The Professor eventually introduced himself and we carried on.

To the other boys it was probably just a bit of a laugh, but to me it marked a day in my life that affected me for many years. It screamed, 'you are useless, you can't speak in public, you have no confidence and you will never amount to anything.' I couldn't understand why this had happened, but it affected me greatly for many years until I discovered a secret to confidence, which I will share later in this chapter.

I call it a secret because, since I discovered it, I now speak with great confidence to hundreds of people – and more importantly than that, I get a great buzz out of it. The more I speak, the more confident I become and those negative voices in my head are completely silent.

It is a great privilege to be able to motivate and inspire people from the stage. To help them gain confidence, to believe in themselves and understand that they can achieve more than they can imagine, with the right mindset. It took me many years to understand why I had that 'meltdown' introducing the professor, and I realised it stems from my childhood and my parents.

Being raised by Polish parents, and because they spoke Polish and no English, I could only speak Polish in my early years. When I got to school as a 5-year-old, I found it very difficult to make friends and communicate with anyone as I couldn't speak a word of English.

Things were very difficult for me in that period of my life and the worst times were those where we all had to practise our reading by standing up one at a time to read out of a book. I remember very well the fear of standing up knowing that I would stumble over the words and that my fellow pupils would snigger and laugh at me as I tried to read to the best of my ability.

Every time I stood up and read, I would hear those sniggers and laughs. My heart would sink and I would feel humiliated, useless and embarrassed. Each of these situations 'put another nail in the coffin' of my confidence. I was gradually establishing a 'negative anchor' to the event which would come back to haunt me years later as I introduced the Professor.

This negative anchor was so strong that it brought back all the emotions I felt as that humiliated young boy in class. My inner voice was so negative that it was taking over my thinking process and was so loud that I couldn't think of anything else including introducing the Professor.

"You can't fall if you don't climb. But there's no joy in living your whole life on the ground."

Unknown

The Confidence Formula

When I was around 30 years of age, after I had finished playing basketball professionally, I joined a local radio station called Metro FM and TFM. I was a regional sales executive selling radio airtime to companies across the country. I was still a very nervous person when speaking in front of more than one person. In this role with the radio station, I had to make presentations to around 10 people on a regular basis and I was a nervous wreck.

Luckily for me, one significant day, a sales director from the station called Harry Dunne took me to one side and gave me some advice that quite simply changed my life. He gave me a very simple three-step formula to improve my confidence in public speaking, and since that time I have become better and better.

That negative anchor was broken and I now live free from the negative inner voices that were destroying me. I will be forever grateful to Harry, who cared enough to share this secret with me that changed my life dramatically. Without this intervention I would not be running my business, changing people's lives for the better – in effect, helping others like Harry helped me.

There is a very simple three-step process to the confidence formula and I will share this with you right here, right now. The following technique works best if you do this about a week before the pressure event you are working towards. The more you practise these techniques before the event, the better you will perform.

Step One: Visualisation – Inside your body
You see yourself in the situation where you are going to perform under pressure from inside your body. This means that if you are preparing to make a presentation to 20 people in a boardroom setting, in this first step you see them in front of you in clear detail. You see them as you would want them to respond to the best presentation they have ever seen. You see them smiling at the right times, very attentive, nodding in agreement, looking at each other with that knowing look of 'this is good.' They may be applauding at the end and shaking you by the hand when it has finished. Use the techniques described in chapter 13 on Visualisation.

Step Two: Visualisation – Outside your body
Next you see yourself from the other people's point of view. You see yourself standing up and performing really well. You are speaking perfectly, all the words are coming out well, and your body language is positive with calm, open gestures and a confident posture. You see yourself looking great, really healthy, full of energy, and you can see that you are enjoying this. You are dressed very smartly, you are calm and you have great composure.

Step Three: Inner Voice
The inner voice is that very powerful self-talk that can make or break us. We all have an inner dialogue that never ceases and it can be negative or positive. If your inner voice is positive, you will perform well. If it is negative, you won't. The inner voice is like the rudder of a ship; it is only very small and mainly unnoticed, but it has the power to steer your life. By controlling your inner voice you can change the way your respond to many things. The more positive your inner voice becomes, the more positive your outlook will become.

The way to develop a positive inner voice for stressful situations is to develop a few very short phrases that you can repeat over and over to dispel any negative thoughts you are having. The mind can only think of one thing at a time, so if you are thinking negatively about an upcoming presentation you can change the thinking process. Do this by repeating over and over the four or five phrases you have developed.

My inner voice statements for public speaking used to be, 'oh no, I'm useless at this,' 'I will forget what to say,' 'they will laugh at me,' 'I'll get it wrong as I always do,' and 'I hate standing up in front of people.'

Now things are so different because my inner voice is positive and more confident. Examples of my inner dialogue now are, 'I can't wait,' 'I'm excited,' 'I was born for this,' and 'Bring it on!'

What a difference in my self-talk and because of this my presentations are getting better and better each time I deliver them. I achieve this by visualising the outcome I want, both from seeing the audience from my point of view, and seeing me from the audience's point of view. I also develop a positive inner voice to use both before and during the presentation.

The inner voice can also destroy you during the presentation, not just before you start. In the past, you may have experienced the awareness of being able to hear yourself speaking inside your head at the same time as you are actually making the presentation. This is a very weird experience but when you are very nervous during the presentation you will hear yourself saying things to yourself. Things like, 'see that man has his arms folded – he hates it,' or 'the audience is very quiet so they can't be enjoying it.' The fact is that they could be so riveted that they are taking in every word!

Our job is to maintain a positive inner voice during the entire presentation. By learning a series of short phrases, you simply repeat these whenever the negative voice appears.

"Too many of us are not living our dreams because we are living our fears."

Les Brown

Summary

- Confidence allows you to perform well under pressure.
- Your level of confidence can be improved and developed.
- It shows in your body language, speech and reactions to different situations.
- Confident people are more positive and have a strong self-belief.
- Self-belief is essential – it is the opinion you have of yourself.
- Negative experiences in childhood can contribute to feelings of weak self-belief.
- A 'negative anchor' can affect you for many years.
- Remember to use The Confidence Formula.
- Visualise the audience responding as you want them to.
- Visualise yourself performing as you want to.
- Develop a set of phrases to replace the negative voice.

"Trust yourself. Create the kind of self that you will be happy to live with all your life. Make the most of yourself by fanning the tiny, inner sparks of possibility into flames of achievement."

Golda Meir

Action Plan

Practise these techniques before your next stressful event. This technique works for any stressful situation, both work-related and personal. It could be a dinner party, an interview, or meeting someone special for the first time.

For a presentation at work:

Step One
Visualise the event in detail before you get there. Refer to chapter 13 on Visualisation for the specific techniques involved. Make sure you see the audience in detail and exactly how you want them to respond. Do this two or three times a day for about a week before the event if you have that time available. If not, do it for as many days or hours as you have available.

Step Two
Visualise yourself from the point of view of the audience and see yourself looking poised, happy, confident, healthy, energised, speaking slowly and clearly, with a positive, open body language. Do this for seven days prior to the event, or for as many days as you have available.

Step Three
Develop between four to five brief phrases that you can learn and own. You need to really believe the statements; don't develop one that you don't really believe, otherwise it won't work. You have to believe that you can become what you are saying. You don't have to be there yet but you do need to believe that you can get there.

I have produced a list of over 70 inner voice statements, which I have collated during my Confidence Building workshops. If you e-mail me, I will happily send you a copy of these so you can either use some of them directly or adapt them to suit your personality.

Final Thoughts

You can live the life you want and be happy and successful, but like anything in life, you have to really believe you can achieve what you want. That self-belief is the power base of energy that you were born with, and it is from this that your confidence grows.

Using simple but powerful techniques of self-talk and visualisation, you will be able to alter and improve your confidence levels in all aspects of your life.

"Believe in yourself! Have faith in your abilities! Without a humble but reasonable confidence in your own powers, you cannot be successful or happy."

Norman Vincent Peale

Focus

Intensely paying attention to a single object, concept, person or activity, to the exclusion of everything else

Chapter 5

Focus – the fifth key pillar

Intensely paying attention to a single object, concept, person or activity, to the exclusion of everything else

Introduction

Focus is your ability to centre your attention and energy on a specific task, object or activity for a sustained length of time. If you want to succeed in life, if you want to get what you desire most, if you want to achieve your goals, you need to master the art of focus.

This doesn't only apply to succeeding in your business, in your career, or improving your financial situation. It stands true for every aspect of your life including finding more fulfilment, forming better relationships, improving your health, and learning new skills.

When you focus on short-term tasks and goals, your motivation levels remain high because you see results quickly. However, it is much more difficult to focus on goals that might take months, years or even decades to achieve. One reason for this is that you may lose sight of what you wanted to achieve, and more importantly why you wanted to achieve that goal.

With longer-term goals, it can also be difficult to recognise and measure progress, especially in the early stages. Therefore, it is easy to get distracted by other projects that seem more exciting and which are usually shorter-term priorities. However, the ability to focus in the long term is a key skill for anyone who wants to be successful, particularly for leaders who want to inspire their teams to achieve a future vision.

"The person who says it cannot be done should not interrupt the person who is doing it."

Chinese Proverb

What is Focus?

Reaching and maintaining a state of 'laser-like focus' takes practise and discipline. It is something that should always be at the back of your mind and a part of you should always be able to see yourself as having already achieved your goal. As you practice this, with time, you will develop a personal guidance system that will instantly warn you if you start moving away from your goal, so that you can get back on track.

People often think they are focused, but in most cases they are not. They may be working on an important task, but often their minds are roaming and they are thinking about something else. They may even be checking their emails every 20 minutes, or getting distracted by all sorts of things that are going on around them.

Laser-like focus means all your thoughts, feelings, beliefs and actions are fully aligned with your goal all day long – day in, day out. There is no point wanting to succeed financially yet holding on to beliefs like 'money is evil' or 'money corrupts people,' or even the idea that you'll never be rich because you don't have enough education. Your focus needs to become your life attitude, so your belief system is critical.

"Whenever you want to achieve something, keep your eyes open, concentrate and make sure you know exactly what it is you want. No one can hit their target with their eyes closed."

Paulo Coelho

Story

An ancient sage was teaching his disciples the art of archery. He put a wooden bird as the target and asked them to aim at the eye of the bird. The first disciple was asked to describe what he saw. He said, 'I see the trees, the branches, the leaves, the sky, the bird and its eye.' The sage asked this disciple to shoot and he missed. Then he asked the second disciple the same question and he replied, 'I only see the eye of the bird.' The sage said, 'very good, then shoot.' The arrow went straight and hit the eye of the bird.

What is the moral of the story? Unless we focus, we cannot achieve our goal.

I spend a great deal of time travelling around the country by car or train. When I travel to London to coach my clients, I book a first class seat to make sure I have the peace I need to work effectively for those couple of hours I have. It may seem a bit extravagant to travel first class, but it is most certainly worth the extra cost as the amount of great work I get done is amazing.

Instead of seeing the journey as something I have to suffer, I now really look forward to the journey where I have time and space to focus on things that are important. I find that I am very creative during this journey, so I often leave some of the most strategic planning for this time.

When I get to London, I use the time on the Tube to check a few things for my coaching session so I am fully prepared. After the coaching session, I get the Tube back to the mainline station and go straight to a tea shop where I e-mail my coaching client with a summary of the meeting. I then answer a few e-mails, and make sure I time my walk to the train so that I can walk straight to my seat.

On the journey back I start by reading a newspaper for about 15 minutes then get my laptop out and start work again. As the tea is brought to me I am engrossed in a few e-mails or other productive work until I arrive back in Nottingham. The difference with this focused attitude is not only that I get a lot of great work done, but the time flies by and I'm at my destination before I know it.

"Lack of direction, not lack of time, is the problem. We all have twenty-four hour days."

Zig Ziglar

Developing Focus

It can be hard to focus and concentrate, but it is a skill that can be learned. There are strategies that can help to build the motivation and persistence you need to achieve your long-term objectives.

- **Identify Specific Long-Term Goals**
  Get an absolutely clear vision of what you want – what excites you? What draws you? Find your passion in life and align your long-term goals with this. If you are following your dreams, it will be much easier to devote all your energies towards achieving your goals; you will naturally be drawn towards focusing on them.

  Set specific long-term goals for the important areas of your life, such as career, finances, family and education.

- **Create a Plan of Action**
  Once you have identified your goals, write them down as a physical commitment to yourself. Depending on

their complexity you may need to do some research to identify the required steps to achieve these goals. The first plan may not be perfect, but it will be good enough to get started and you can adapt it as you go along. The stronger your focus grows, the more strategies, action steps and ideas will flow into your mind.

Word your goals in a way that communicates why they are important to you and put them in a place where you will see them regularly. Write them on index cards that you can keep in a wallet or purse, or print them on a sheet of paper and stick it on a wall where you will see it frequently. Set a reminder to spend a few minutes looking at your goals every day to maintain your focus.

- **Identify Your Most Important Tasks**
  Focus on the most important habits, thought patterns and action steps that provide the quickest way to your goal. To do this, you need to identify the most important steps and tasks to focus on and ruthlessly ignore anything that is not aligned with your goal.

  This is known as 'The Eisenhower Principle', as the U.S. President was said to live his life by it. Using a tool such as the Urgent / Important Matrix, we can determine which tasks we need to do and which can be delegated or scrapped. This frees up our time to focus on activities that contribute to our long-term goals.

The Eisenhower Box

	Urgent	Not Urgent
Impprtant	I (MANAGE) • Crisis • Medical emergencies • Pressing problems • Deadline-driven projects • Last-minute preparations for scheduled activities	II (FOCUS) • Preparation/planning • Prevention • Values clarification • Exercise • Relationship-building • True recreation/relaxation
	Quadrant of Necessity	Quadrant of Quality & Personal Leadership
Not Important	III (AVOID) • Interruptions, some calls • Some mail & reports • Some meetings • Many "pressing" matters • Many popular activities	IV (AVOID) • Trivia, busywork • Junk mail • Some phone messages/email • Time wasters • Escape activities • Viewing mindless TV shows
	Quadrant of Deception	Quadrant of Waste

'What is important is seldom urgent and what is urgent is seldom Important.'

Dwight Eisenhower, 34th President of the United States

Eisenhower recognised that great time management means being effective as well as efficient. In other words, we must spend our time on things that are important and not just the ones that are urgent. To do this and to reduce the stress of having too many tight deadlines, we need to understand this distinction:

- **Important** activities have an outcome that leads to us achieving our goals, either professional or personal.

- **Urgent** activities demand immediate attention and are usually associated with achieving other people's goals. They demand our attention and are often the ones we concentrate on because the consequences of not dealing with them are immediate.

It is vital that we know which activities are important and which are urgent, so that we can overcome the natural tendency to focus on unimportant urgent activities. This can clear enough time to do what is essential for our success. This is the way to move from 'fire fighting' into a position where we can grow our businesses and our careers.

- **Strengthen Self-Regulation**
  This is the ability to control our emotions and impulses and is said to be a very important factor in achieving our long-term goals. To develop it we need to work on our self-discipline, which will keep us working hard towards our goals even when not 'in the mood' to do it.

  Another important factor in self-regulation is self-efficacy, which is the belief in your ability to reach your goals and involves working on your self-confidence. Confidence is covered in Chapter 4.

- **Recognise Progress**
  Your long-term goals might not be achieved for years or even decades, so it is important to recognise and celebrate the small steps along the way. Each day, take a few minutes to look at your progress towards your goal and congratulate yourself for what you have achieved, even if there are no hugely meaningful results. It is helpful to think about what you have learned, rather than about what you have achieved, when reviewing your progress.

  For bigger milestones, make a point of rewarding yourself with something significant, such as a meal with your partner or a day out. Recognising your achievements will make it easier to maintain your long-term focus.

- **Avoid Distractions**
  We are all different and what is a distraction to one person may be natural for another. For example, reading with a TV on in the background. It is important to identify your own triggers of distraction and eliminate them in order to help you focus when you need to.

  In my case, I find it much easier to concentrate when there is noise in the background rather than when there is silence. Because of this, when I'm not training, speaking or coaching I spend my days working in tea shops. I have identified about eight great tea shops that I frequent when I am working on my business. This also gives me a great opportunity to get to know the staff at each place, and this makes it an even more pleasant experience. I know which ones I can go to when it is lunchtime or when it is sunny; it gives me the flexibility to choose the ideal working environment for me.

"Do what you can, where you are, with what you have."

Teddy Roosevelt

Why do we Break Focus?

Science has identified two main external triggers that cause people to break focus – loud noises and blinking lights. Minimising these common distractions is a sure way to ensure no outside forces will break your focus. A simple way of doing this is to wear noise-cancelling headphones or earplugs to eliminate noise.

Noise comes in various forms such as someone calling your name, a car backfiring or a motorbike revving up along the road, any of which is enough to break your focus. To prevent other distractions, you can remove visual cues from your environment, which usually involves blocking audio and visual notifications on your computer.

As for your internal distractions, you need to learn to pinpoint them and stop them before they start. We all get distracted by different thoughts throughout the day, especially when our mind is not in the present moment. Those thoughts might be about all the other tasks you need to do next, or maybe what you're going to be eating for dinner.

However, you can limit these brain wanderings when you need to focus on a task by simply putting the brakes on the thought process. It is not easy to do, but it's possible to stop those thoughts from overwhelming you. This has been described as 'paying attention to your attention'.

Summary

- Focus is your ability to centre your attention and energy on a specific task, object or activity for a sustained length of time.
- Short-term goals are easier to focus on.
- With longer-term goals, it can be difficult to recognise and measure progress.
- Reaching and maintaining a state of 'laser-like focus' takes practice and discipline
- Focus allows you to shut out distractions so that you can work persistently to achieve a desired state or goal.
- To develop long-term focus, set meaningful goals that you'll enjoy working towards and write them down.
- Develop a step plan of action to achieve those goals.
- Do tasks according to their relevance in the 'Urgent/ Important Matrix'
- Stay on course by not acting impulsively on new ideas.
- Strengthen your self-discipline, and develop the good

habits you'll need to move towards your goals in the months and years to come.

- Learn to recognise and celebrate the progress you make, day to day.
- Avoid external and internal distractions.

Action Plan

Set your personal levels of focus:

1. **Lifetime** – A lifetime focus means having a purpose for your life.
   Make a lifetime 'mission statement': What are your passions? What really matters to you?
2. **Yearly** – After making a lifetime focus, make a yearly focus.
   Your yearly focus must relate to your lifetime focus. Focus on one or two major, specific and measurable goals during the year.
3. **Weekly** – Set your weekly goals at the start of the week. What do you want to achieve by the end of this week? Your weekly goals should relate to your yearly and lifetime goals.
4. **Daily** – Each morning set your goals for the day.
   Make one goal your most important task and focus on it until it is complete. Keep a to-do list and keep checking it to stay focused.
5. **Currently** – Stay focused whenever you are working on any task.
   Avoid distractions and multi-tasking to maintain focus. Accomplish as much as you can.

Final Thoughts

If you want to succeed in life, if you want to get what you desire most, if you want to achieve your goals, you need to master the art of focus.

We all struggle to maintain focus in our daily lives. Endless distractions keep our brains from focusing on a task as we struggle to get things done at work and complete projects around the house.

Laser-like focus takes practice and the more you do it, the stronger it will become.

"What fires together wires together."

Donald Hebb, Canadian Neuropsychologist

Positive Inner Voice

Our inner voices are embedded in our earliest childhood experiences and are reinforced throughout childhood, adolescence, and into adulthood

Chapter 6

Developing a Positive Inner Voice

Our inner voices are embedded in our earliest childhood experiences and are reinforced throughout childhood, adolescence, and into adulthood

Introduction

We have an inner voice that speaks to us consciously and unconsciously all the time. Our self-esteem and self-image are developed by how we talk to ourselves. When our inner voice becomes critical, it drags us down until we cannot have adequate love or esteem for ourselves.

"We are what we think about all day long."

Ralph Waldo Emerson

Everyone has an inner critic. All of us have conscious and unconscious memories of all the times we felt bad or wrong – they are part of the unavoidable scars of childhood. This is where the critical inner voice gets started.

An internal voice may remind us of past failures, sorrows or disappointments, torture us with criticism or verbal abuse, describe frightening or unpleasant futures, or disturb us in other ways.

The critical inner voice is the part of us that is turned against ourselves. It is the defended, negative side of our personality that is opposed to our on-going development. It is a hostile, judgemental advisor.

Effects of the Critical Inner Voice:

- It creates a negative, pessimistic picture of the world.
- It undermines our ability to interpret events realistically.
- It attacks our mood, psychological state of mind, attitudes and prejudices.
- It damages personal relationships and style of relating to others.
- It affects the choice of school or career and work performance.
- It consists of the negative thoughts, beliefs and attitudes that oppose our best interests.
- It encourages and strongly influences self-defeating and self-destructive behaviour.
- It warns us about other people, promoting angry and cynical attitudes toward others.
- It triggers negative moods and sabotages our pursuit of satisfaction and meaning in life.
- It leads to a sense of alienation; a feeling of being removed from ourselves and distant from others.

The critical inner voice exists to varying degrees in every person. It is not an auditory hallucination; it is experienced as thoughts within your head. If we hear its destructive point of view and believe what it is telling us, we will fail to challenge it and instead we will act on it. This process has a seriously negative consequence on our lives.

The critical inner voice is not a conscience or a moral guide. What most distinguishes the inner voice from a conscience is its degrading, punishing quality. Its demeaning tone tends to increase our feelings of self-hatred instead of motivating us to change undesirable actions in a constructive manner. You don't have to look far to find your critical inner voice, for example:

- It is there when you go to a job interview: "Why are you wasting your time? The other applicants are more qualified for this job."

- It is there when you express a point of view: "You idiot, why did you say that? Now everyone will think you are stupid."
- It is there when you make a mistake: "Can't you do anything right? You are embarrassing yourself!"
- These thoughts can be cruel and berating: "Who do you think you are? You'll never succeed. You're not like everyone else. No one will ever care about you."
- These thoughts can also be deceptively calm and soothing: "You're just fine on your own. The only person you can rely on is yourself. You should reward yourself with one more piece of cake. Just have one last drink; it will make you feel better."

We can observe this voice at work in various areas of our lives; it tells us not to get too close in our relationships or go too far in our careers. Whether cruel or soothing, these thoughts often hold us back from going after what we want and lead to our acting in ways that hurt us. Giving in to the voice and acting on its advice only creates more attacks – the voice that told us to have that extra piece of cake is now ridiculing us for having no self-control.

The critical inner voice reveals itself in those little everyday thoughts that flit through our consciousness, which are here and gone before we are even fully aware of them. Though sometimes hard to pinpoint, the inner voice is often experienced as a running commentary that attacks and criticises our actions and interactions in everyday life.

"Don't let the noise of others' opinions drown out your own inner voice."

Steve Jobs

If we all listened to these negative people, then some of the greatest life stories would never happen. Take this for example:

George Lucas spent four years sending the script for Star Wars around to the various studios and collecting numerous rejections in the process. If he'd let his negative inner voice get to him, he would never have ended up having the highest grossing film of all time. Think of all the great Lucas movies we might never have seen if he'd let those rejections get to him.

Developing a Positive Inner Voice is vital to developing Mental Resilience – without commanding positive self-talk it is not possible to be positive and happy.

Story

A few weeks ago I had the biggest challenge I have ever faced to date: my first ever TV interview. It was to be recorded at Zen TV, an up and coming internet TV station, to be broadcast a few weeks later.

I am a regular on BBC Radio Nottingham as a newspaper reviewer and really enjoy it. I was a touch nervous when I read my first review, but the inner voice remained positive and it went well. I believe I have improved with each review. Recently I was interviewed on both BBC Radio Nottingham and also on BBC Radio Derby. These were eight-minute and 15-minute interviews that were at the next level of pressure.

It has intrigued me how I have maintained confidence on each of these occasions, as well as at the keynote talks I deliver to several hundred people. The old me used to get so nervous that I would stumble over words, look nervous and wouldn't perform well at all. I was basically self-

sabotaging with a self-fulfilling prophecy.

Then I discovered the power of the inner voice and I started to develop a positive inner dialogue. The more I concentrated on this, the more positive my thoughts became. I found that I could get rid of negative thoughts very quickly and replace them with positive ones. I realised that I had a choice between positive and negative inner dialogue. The more I practised this, the more positive I became.

I turned up at the TV studio with Julie and sat with a cup of tea for about 20 minutes before we were called into the studio. I sat on the couch and was introduced to G-Man, who was going to interview me.

We had a chat and he introduced me to the team around me. There were three cameras, seven people and a photographer.

I sat back and relaxed. I had visualised this scene for a few days before and had kept all negative thoughts out of my head, only allowing positive dialogue to take place. This is something I have worked on and it has improved as the time has gone by.

As the time approached to start the interview I wasn't rehearsing anything in my head. I was simply relaxing and trusting that when the questions were asked the answers would come to me easily and effortlessly. I have found that if I analyse and think ahead too much I get things mixed up and it doesn't flow naturally – this is the same for my keynote talks.

We were counted down from three to one and we were on camera. G-Man introduced me and asked the first question and we were off. The answers came easily and effortlessly and I thoroughly enjoyed the experience. I had a positive inner voice going on in my head and this kept me on track and happy.

Towards the end, he asked if I could spin the ball on my finger or whether it was a prop and I said that I could spin the ball and that we would see if I could. The pressure point came as I attempted to spin the ball on my finger first time and I did. It spun for quite a while causing G-Man to realise that it was clearly not a prop.

I passed this pressure test because my inner voice was positive so my body was relaxed and this helped with the basketball spin.

The change for me over the years has been nothing short of amazing. I developed from being the 18-year old who couldn't talk in front of anyone, to the keynote speaker who addresses hundreds of people from the stage with confidence. I have also been interviewed on local radio and local TV stations, again with no difficulty.

"Believing in negative thoughts is the single greatest obstruction to success."

Charles F. Glassman

Developing a Positive Inner Voice

If I was asked to name the single most important technique I have used to develop my Mental Resilience it would have to be developing a positive inner voice. This seems to work really well, and is a life changer for many people once they learn the techniques involved.

Positive self-talk usually consists of words or brief phrases that inspire, motivate, or remind us to focus and keep moving. Phrases like, 'keep your head down,' 'let's go,' and, 'breathe,' help us focus our attention and trigger the hopefully ideal response and action for the task at hand. Some of my positive inner voice phrases when I feel overwhelmed are, 'just do one thing at a time.' 'I can do it,' 'I'm good at this,' 'I'm excited,' and, 'bring it on!'

Reminding myself to pause and inhale before I deal with a difficult situation often keeps me focused on the task.

"If you hear a voice within you say "you cannot paint," then by all means paint and that voice will be silenced."

Vincent Van Gogh

Summary

- We have an inner voice that speaks to us consciously and unconsciously all the time.
- Our self-esteem and self-image are developed by how we talk to ourselves.
- The critical inner voice is the part of us that is turned against ourselves.
- It is opposed to our on-going development and is a hostile, judgemental advisor.
- It is often experienced as a running commentary that attacks and criticises our actions and interactions in everyday life.
- We need to develop a positive inner voice, which creates positive results.
- Positive self-talk consists of words or brief phrases that inspire, motivate, or remind us to focus and keep moving.
- You have to listen to your heart and do what is best for you in your life.

Action Plan

1. **Notice what you're already saying to yourself**
   Most of us don't give conscious attention to the voices rambling in our heads. Consciously tune into your self-talk; you can't change it if you are not aware of it. Identify an area of your life where you are especially critical of yourself and then pay attention to what the criticisms are.

2. **Articulate the attacks in the second person**
   It is valuable to articulate these self-attacks in the second person, as 'you' statements. For example, instead of saying, 'I feel so lazy and useless,' say, 'you are so lazy. You're useless.' Using this format, the critical thoughts are expressed as they are heard, which often leads to identifying the hostility that underlies this self-attacking system.

3. **Focus on something else**
   Whenever you hear that voice, think of something positive in your life. Think about a loved one or a funny joke, anything to get you back in a positive mindset. Go for a walk – sometimes just doing something physical gives us enough endorphins to actually feel better about ourselves.

4. **Pick your power phrase**
   Pick three of four phrases that feel good. You may even feel a rush of energy when you say them and practise them out loud. Choose words that inspire you, motivate you, make you laugh or boost your mood – for example, 'you are good at this,' or, 'you're the Man!'

5. **Try the Power of Possible Thinking**
   When you're feeling down and force yourself to say

positive things to yourself, you often end up feeling worse, because your internal lie detector goes off.

An alternative is a technique called possible thinking, which involves using neutral thoughts about any situation and naming the facts. For example, 'I'm a fat blob,' becomes, 'I'd like to lose 10 pounds and I know how to do it.' The facts give you a lot more choices and directions you can go in.

6. Embrace your imperfections

It's enormously freeing to stop holding yourself to ridiculously high standards. Perfectionism is destructive. Interviews with successful CEOs and award-winning athletes found that they credit their success to a willingness to make mistakes and move on, rather than consistently trying to be perfect.

7. Put negative stuff in a box

When we're being attacked by negativity, a tiny blunder is inflated into a huge failure. So the next time a negative thought intrudes, take a few deep breaths and then quickly narrow it down and put your problems into the smallest imaginary box possible.

Seeing a tiny box in your mind shows the actual size of the problem and helps you feel more confident that you can take it on. Put the worry in a small box on the top shelf of the cupboard in your mind and pack it away.

8. Take small steps

Instead of getting frustrated because you keep being attacked, just keep doing whatever it is that you love doing. You'll find that you're happiest then. This will encourage you to keep going.

Final Thoughts

Usually somewhere along the way we came across someone who told us that we're not good at doing something, and we believe them. It could be anything: writing, singing, dancing or speaking. The tragedy comes from not following our dreams because we always hear that one negative voice telling us that we're no good. No matter how many other people tell us the opposite, we always remember that one negative voice.

Life is too short to not do the things we love because some misguided person told us not to do it. If you love singing, then sing. How about writing? If you love it, do it. That's the only reason - it brings you joy, so do it. You have to listen to your heart and do what is best for you.

Remember when you finally do succeed that most negative person who said you could never do it will probably be the loudest person to say, 'I knew they could do it.' It's human nature.

It's your life, not someone else's. So, LIVE IT

"Stop focusing so much on what is on the outside and start getting to know yourself better on the inside. Your true purpose in life lies in your inner positive voices."

Edmond Mbiaka

Positive Mindset

A positive mental attitude is the belief that one can increase achievement through optimistic thought processes

Chapter 7

Developing a Positive Mindset

A positive mental attitude is the belief that one can increase achievement through optimistic thought processes

Introduction

What is positive thinking? Positive thinking is an umbrella term for a range of ideas and techniques associated with the psychology of achievement. It is the main idea that lies behind the self-help movement that originated in the United States and has since become very influential worldwide.

More and more people, including doctors and scientists, are turning to positive thinking because it is a powerful tool for transforming your inner self into a remarkable health-generating and self-healing entity. Optimistic people have discovered that the human mind has the power to turn wishes into reality through positive thinking and developing a positive mindset.

All of our feelings, beliefs and knowledge are based on our internal thoughts, both conscious and subconscious, and we are in control of these processes. We can choose to be positive or negative, enthusiastic or dull, active or passive. These choices influence our feelings and behaviour, and they can also impact on our physical health.

Such choices are habits, developed over a lifetime and shaped by the feedback of parents, friends, teachers and colleagues, and also by our own self-talk. They are maintained by the inner conversations we have with ourselves, both consciously and subconsciously.

The first step in developing a positive mindset is to change our inner conversations. If we can learn to think more optimistically about events and situations, we are more likely to be happy and achieve success.

"Life is 10% what happens to me and 90% of how I react to it."

Charles Swindoll

Positive thinking is an optimistic state of mind that always sees the bright side of life and focuses on the glass being half full instead of half empty. It is a mental attitude that produces constructive results – it brings inner satisfaction, peace and better health, improves relationships and attracts success into your life. Whilst we all have this powerful tool, many of us are not aware of it.

Researchers continue to find increasing evidence pointing to the many benefits of positive thinking. According to a Stanford Research Institute study, success is 88% positive thinking, and only 12% education. Therefore, positive thinking is an important factor in your ability to succeed in life.

Top sports coaches believe that positive mental attitudes are every bit as important as physical fitness. An increasing number of health practitioners believe that physical ailments can be better addressed through positive thinking rather than conventional medicine. Positive psychology also forms an important part of training programmes in commerce and industry.

Story

Alan applied for a new job, but he didn't believe he would get it since his self-esteem was low, and he considered himself as a failure and unworthy of success. He had a negative attitude and, therefore, believed that the other applicants were better and more qualified than him.
For the whole week preceding the job interview, Alan's mind was occupied with negative thoughts and fears concerning the job. He actually anticipated failure.

On the day of the interview, he got up late, and to his horror he discovered that the shirt he planned to wear was dirty and the other one needed ironing. As it was already too late, he went out wearing a wrinkled shirt and without eating breakfast.

During the interview, he was tense, negative, hungry and worried about his shirt. All this distracted his mind and made it difficult for him to focus on the interview. His overall behaviour made a bad impression, and consequently, his fear materialised and he did not get the job.

Jim applied for the same job too, but approached the matter in a different way. He was sure that he was going to get the job. During the week preceding the interview, he often visualised himself making a good impression and getting the job.

In the evening before the interview, he prepared the clothes he was going to wear and went to sleep a little earlier. On day of the interview, he woke up earlier than usual and had ample time to eat breakfast, then to arrive to the interview before the scheduled time. Jim made a good impression and got the job.

What do we learn from these two stories? Positive thinking, accompanied by appropriate actions, will naturally bring about more achievement and success.

"When one door of happiness closes, another opens, but often we look so long at the closed door that we do not see the one that has been opened for us."

Helen Keller

Studies

Some long-term studies on positive thinking and health suggest the evidence so far affirms that positive thinking leads to positive outcomes.

One of the most prominent advocates of positive thinking is Professor Martin Seligman – an American psychologist famous for his work on learned optimism. His work emphasises happiness rather than success and he believes that optimism is one of the most important factors. What matters, he argues, is the way that people interpret what happens to them and how they think about a positive or negative event in their lives.

According to Seligman, when faced with an event where something negative happens, people can choose to place either a temporary or a permanent frame around it. People have an internal dialogue where they might say to themselves, 'this is my fault. It's going to get worse and there is nothing I can do about it. It will last forever.'

Others, however, might say, 'what happened was out of my control. The situation is only temporary and I can change things for the better.'

The reverse holds for when people experience good events;

the pessimistic thinker views the effects as temporary, whereas the optimistic thinker will embrace the positive situation and place a permanent frame around it. Seligman's believes that optimistic learners achieve more both during their school years and also throughout their lives.

"You can never cross the ocean until you have the courage to lose sight of the shore."

Christopher Columbus

Learned Optimism

Seligman's extensive research across a number of sectors and industries shows that people who have an optimistic mindset are much more able to overcome barriers to learning and persevere until learning outcomes are achieved. Pessimistic learners, by contrast, internalise failure and usually stop trying.

We can learn to be optimistic and to change the nature of our internal dialogue so that we react positively to events, regardless of whether they are good or bad. By changing our habitual vocabulary, we can change the way we think and feel and consequently achieve more positive outcomes. The use of positive language is an integral part of learned optimism programmes.

Seligman believes that optimistic self-talk (internal dialogue) is the key to developing persistence – the ability not to give up in the face of failure – in order to achieve success.

If you have been exhibiting a negative attitude and expecting failure and difficulties, it is now time to change the way you think. It is time to get rid of negative thoughts and behaviour, and start leading a happier and more successful life. If you tried to do so in the past and failed, it only means that you have not tried enough. Perseverance is key and worthwhile.

Benefits of Positive Thinking

A positive attitude manifests in the following ways:

- Positive thinking.
- Constructive thinking.
- Creative thinking.
- Optimism.
- Motivation and energy to do things and accomplish goals.
- An attitude of happiness.

A positive frame of mind can help you in many ways, such as:

- Helping you to expect success and not failure.
- Making you feel inspired.
- Giving you the strength not to give up if you encounter obstacles on your way.
- Making you look at failure and problems as blessings in disguise.
- Believing in yourself and in your abilities.
- Enabling you to show self-esteem and confidence.
- Making you look for solutions, instead of dwelling on problems.
- Making you recognise opportunities.
- Helping you achieve goals and attain success.
- Bringing more happiness into your life.
- Helping you to produce more energy.
- Giving you the ability to inspire and motivate yourself and others.
- Encountering fewer obstacles and difficulties in your daily life.
- Getting more respect and love from people.

Health benefits of positive thinking include:

- Lowering stress levels.
- Improving your body's immune system.
- Making you more resilient and to develop the ability to

overcome life's difficulties.
- Bringing more happiness and respect from other people.
- Increasing your life span.
- Creating greater inner strength to inspire and motivate yourself and others.
- Reducing depression.

"Most folks are as happy as they make up their minds to be."

Abraham Lincoln

I spotted this article in the papers this week and it is a story of an amazing woman who is a driving instructor at 95 years of age! This is a great way to demonstrate the power of a positive mindset.

Story

Britain's oldest driving instructor has passed her 95th birthday and has no plans to stop.

Laura Thomas has got 1,000 pupils through the test over 76 years. She started driving in 1938 when her brother bought her a car for Christmas.

Laura passed her test two months later and started giving her friends tips on how they could do the same. Mother-of-two Laura's reputation spread by word of mouth and she was bombarded by requests for driving lessons.

The great-grandmother has never advertised her services but has enjoyed a steady stream of customers for almost eight decades. She has also never used dual controls in her car and never had an accident. Laura said she had taught nearly 'all the drivers' in Pembroke Dock, West Wales –

> *and none needed more than two tests.*
>
> *She is aiming to join Britain's exclusive '100 club' of centenarians who are still on the roads and says you're never too old to drive along as you have your 'head screwed on.'*
>
> *Widow Laura has no plans to hang up her L-plates and can still reduce teenagers to tears with her 'old school' teaching technique.*

This is a great example of the Power of a Positive Mindset. Not only is Laura still driving at 95 years of age, but she is still teaching people to drive! It's quite amazing, and with her positive mindset I can see her driving for years to come.

Summary

- Positive thinking is a range of ideas and techniques associated with the psychology of achievement.
- It is a powerful tool for transforming your inner self into a health-generating and self-healing entity.
- All of our feelings, beliefs and knowledge are based on our internal thoughts and we are in control of these processes.
- We can choose to be positive or negative, enthusiastic or dull, active or passive.
- Such choices are habits, developed over a lifetime and shaped by the feedback of others and also by our own self-talk.
- We must change our inner conversations and learn to think optimistically.
- Positive thinking is an optimistic state of mind.
- It brings inner satisfaction, peace and better health, improves relationships and attracts success into your life.
- Positive thinkers visualise what they want to happen, not what they wish to avoid.
- They are able to develop a mindset that empowers, rather

than limits, their potential.

- Positive thinking stresses action – we learn and develop by doing what needs to be done, by moving to where we want to be in the future.

Action Plan

When you feed your mind with positive affirmations, information, books, conversations, and audio programs, you develop a more positive attitude and personality. You become more influential and persuasive. You enjoy greater confidence and self-esteem.

Mental fitness is like physical fitness. You develop high levels of self-esteem and a positive attitude with training and practice. Here are seven steps to becoming a completely positive person:

Step One – Positive Affirmations
Speak to yourself positively; control your inner dialog. Use positive affirmations phrased in the positive, present, and personal tense, such as, 'I like myself,' 'I can do it,' 'I feel terrific,' and 'I am responsible!'

Your mind is like a garden. If you do not deliberately plant flowers and tend carefully, weeds will grow without any encouragement at all.

Step Two – Positive Visualisation
Perhaps the most powerful ability that you have is the ability to visualise and see your goals as already accomplished. Create a clear, exciting picture of your goal and your ideal life, and replay this picture in your mind over and over. As you 'see' yourself on the inside, you will 'be' on the outside.

Step Three – Positive People
Your choices of the people with whom you live, work, and associate will have more of an impact on your emotions and your success than any other factor. Decide today to associate with positive people, people who are happy and optimistic and who are going somewhere with their lives.

Step Four – Mental Food
Just as your body is healthy to the degree to which you eat nutritious foods, your mind is healthy to the degree to which you feed it with 'mental protein' rather than 'mental candy'. Read books, magazines and articles, watch TV, DVDs or online courses that are educational, inspirational, or motivational. Listen to positive, constructive CDs and audio programs in your car or on your MP3 player.

Step Five – Positive Training and Development
Lifelong learning and personal improvement is what takes you from poverty to affluence and from underachievement to success and financial independence. When you dedicate yourself to learning and growing and becoming more effective in your thoughts and actions, you take complete control of your life. You dramatically increase the speed at which you move upward to greater heights.

Step Six – Positive Health Habits
Take good care of your physical health. Eat healthy, natural and nutritious foods, and eat them sparingly and in proper balance. A nutritional diet will have an immediate, positive effect on your thoughts and feelings.

Resolve to get regular exercise – when you do this, you feel happier and healthier and experience lower levels of stress and fatigue than a person who sits on the couch and watches television all evening. Get enough rest and relaxation. You need to recharge your batteries on a regular basis, especially when you are going through periods of stress or difficulty. Seek balance in your life.

Step Seven – Positive Expectations
Practicing the Law of Attraction is one of the most powerful techniques you can use to become a positive person and to ensure positive outcomes and better results in your life. See the Chapter on the law of attraction in this book to find how to do this.

Your expectations become your own self-fulfilling prophecies. Whatever you expect with confidence seems to come into your life. So expect to be successful. Expect to be popular when you meet new people. Expect to achieve great goals and create a wonderful life for yourself. When you constantly expect good things to happen, you will seldom be disappointed.

"Formal education will make you a living; self-education will make you a fortune."

Jim Rohn

Final Thoughts
Positive thinking is a mental attitude that helps us see the 'silver lining', which causes us to anticipate happiness, joy, health, and favourable results. Effective positive thinking requires focusing on positive thoughts and positive emotions and also taking positive action to bring about favourable outcomes.

The power of positive thinking is about committing yourself to getting the most out of your day – every day. It is about being enthusiastic, keeping your mind focused on important things, developing strategies for dealing with problems and refusing to waste time participating in negative inner dialogues.

Stress Management

Stress is how you feel when the pressure you're under exceeds your ability to cope. It is a state of mental or emotional strain or tension resulting from adverse or demanding circumstances

Chapter 8

Stress Management

Stress is how you feel when the pressure you're under exceeds your ability to cope. It is a state of mental or emotional strain or tension resulting from adverse or demanding circumstances

Introduction

There are very few certainties in this life, but we can be sure that we will experience stress and hardship at some point. Stress may be inevitable, but how we cope with it is our choice. Everyone reacts to stress differently; how you respond to pressure can depend on your personality.

Stress can also have a positive side. A certain level of stress may be necessary (and can even be enjoyable) in order to help you prepare for something – the stress itself helps to keep you alert and focused, for example, when taking an exam, or having to make a presentation in front of an audience.

Our physical reactions to stress are determined by our biological history, in that we needed to respond to sudden dangers that threatened us when we were still hunters and gatherers. At those times, the release of the hormones adrenaline and cortisol caused the 'fight or flight' response to danger and our bodies still react that way today. However, stress in the modern age is rarely remedied by a fight or flight response. So physical exercise can be used as a surrogate to metabolise the excessive stress hormones and restore your body and mind to a calmer, more relaxed state.

"Stress is an ignorant state. It believes that everything is an emergency."

Natalie Goldberg

Story

Liz Tucker is a health and well-being counsellor specialising in stress management. 14 years ago, at the age of 30, she burned out from work related stress.

She had a building company at the time and was working incredibly hard. She would start work at 7AM and often wouldn't finish until 7PM the following day, 36 hours later. She did vast amounts of travelling for business and in the year she burned out she drove over 100,000 miles.

She loved the adrenaline buzz from all the activity and could manage the work at first, but then started regularly working every weekend. When she met her partner, the pressures of trying to see him and keep on top of the work caused it all to start falling apart.

She started feeling deeply tired and very lethargic and one Sunday night she went to bed early because she felt like she was getting a bit of a cold. When she woke on Monday, she couldn't get out of bed – she could move her fingers, head and feet, but had no energy in her arms and legs. The doctor told her she had burned out from too much stress, which shocked her completely. But she had no work-life balance, her diet of junk food had been appalling, and her body had simply shut down in protest.

For the next three months, she couldn't get out of bed and simply slept. Her physical symptoms were bad enough but the mental 'fog' was worse and she was eventually diagnosed with ME. She remained in this state for four years and the doctors had no idea how to help so she decided to make drastic changes herself to her lifestyle.

She started a regime of proper relaxation, taking the time to have a massage or hypnotherapy, and crucially she began to pace herself and not overdo things. She began to eat a healthy diet with more fruit and vegetables and stopped alcohol and caffeine. After 6 months, she was back to normal. She had lots of energy, her skin was better and she didn't have to stay in bed the whole time. She is working really hard again, as a counsellor now, but the difference these days is that she has a work-life balance and knows what to do when things get too stressful.

Effects of Too Much Stress

Everyone reacts to stress in different ways, but there are some common symptoms to look out for. Your symptoms can be psychological, emotional, behavioural or physical, or a mix of these.

Psychological symptoms of stress can include:
- constant worrying
- an inability to concentrate
- seeing only the negative
- memory problems
- hypochondria
- dreading the future.

The emotional effects of stress may include:
- mood swings
- irritability
- an inability to relax
- feeling overwhelmed
- a sense of loneliness

- depression
- low self-esteem
- a loss of sense of humour.

Your **behaviour** could also change and you may:
- eat more or less than usual
- sleep too much or too little
- isolate yourself
- use alcohol, tobacco or illegal drugs to relax;
- develop nervous habits, e.g. nail biting
- find it difficult to concentrate and make decisions
- cry frequently.

Stress can also cause **physical** symptoms:
- aches and pains
- diarrhoea and constipation
- nausea
- chest pains
- headaches
- cramps or muscle spasms
- fainting
- teeth grinding at night
- pins and needles
- high blood pressure
- indigestion.

In this busy modern world, there's always too much to do: yet another deadline; daily meetings; numerous people demanding your attention. There are also things you want to do for yourself too like eating, exercising, sleeping, and getting some relaxation – the stress of all these demands can be devastating if not addressed.

I juggle many roles, each of which demand a great deal of my time – as an author, public speaker, coach, trainer and mentor. I do all this while working to maintain a loving home life and my personal physical, emotional and spiritual health.

It is a huge amount to manage. Stress can easily consume me while I try to squeeze one more thing into my over-busy day. And none of this is eased by the fact that I'm something of a perfectionist, too. It is important to plan each day, with time for work and other tasks, but also making time for relaxation.

"Is everything as urgent as your stress would imply?"

Terri Guillemets

Summary

- We will all get stressed at some point in life.
- Stress can cause psychological, emotional, behavioural or physical problems.
- How we react to pressure and stress is our choice.
- Stress may be destructive but can also have a positive effect by focusing our minds.
- Striking a good work-life balance is essential for optimum functioning.
- There are simple, practical techniques to help reduce stress levels.
- Relaxation and healthy eating are vital to tackling stress.

"The time to relax is when you don't have time for it."

Sydney J. Harris

Action Plan

If your stress is caused by the pressure of being too busy and trying to fit too much into the day, you need to make sure you take time for leisure, exercise and holidays. This is just as essential as spending time on business or home worries. Remember that a little stress is good for the body and alerts the mind. But it needs to be short-term and to be followed by a period of relaxation. Here are some simple tips to manage and reduce your stress levels:

1. **Avoid Caffeine, Alcohol, and Nicotine**
   Caffeine, alcohol and nicotine are stimulants and so will increase your level of stress rather than reduce it. Swap caffeinated and alcoholic drinks for water, herbal teas, or diluted natural fruit juices and aim to keep yourself hydrated as this will enable your body to cope better with stress.

2. **Indulge in Physical Activity**
   Stressful situations increase the level of the stress hormones adrenaline and cortisol in your body. When you feel stressed and tense, go for a brisk walk in fresh air. Have a change of scene – a short walk can make a big difference to how you feel.

   Try to incorporate some physical activity into your daily routine on a regular basis, either before or after work or at lunchtime. Regular physical activity will also improve the quality of your sleep.

3. **Get More Sleep**
   A lack of sleep is a significant cause of stress. However, stress also interrupts our sleep as thoughts keep whirling through our heads, stopping us from relaxing enough to fall asleep. Stop doing any mentally

demanding work several hours before going to bed so that you give your brain time to calm down.

Good sleep techniques are covered in Chapter 18.

4. Try Relaxation Techniques

To manage stress, the first thing is to become more relaxed in daily life. Don't waste energy on things that don't require it; such as fidgeting impatiently while you wait for the kettle to boil. Instead take the opportunity for a few moments of calm.

The second is to learn some breathing and relaxation techniques. Each day, try to relax with a stress reduction technique. There are many tried and tested ways to reduce stress, so try a few and see what works best for you. For example, you could use self-hypnosis words such as, 'calm,' 'peace,' or, 'love'.

Progressive muscle relaxation works really well. This is where you firstly relax your feet, then your calves, then your thighs and then move up the rest of your body until your whole body is relaxed

Try nurturing activities, making time in your life for fun and relaxation:

5. Talk to Someone

Stress can cloud your judgement and prevent you

from seeing things clearly. Talking things through with a friend, work colleague or trained professional can help you find solutions to your stress and put your problems into perspective.

6. Keep a Stress Diary

A stress diary can help you identify the regular stressors in your life and the way you deal with them. Each time you feel stressed, keep track of it in your diary. As you keep a daily log, you will begin to see patterns and common themes that will help you become more aware of the situations that cause you to become stressed. Note the date, time and place of each stressful episode, and write down:

- What caused your stress (make a guess if you're unsure);
- A stress rating of the episode (on a 1 – 10 scale);
- How you felt, both physically and emotionally;
- How you acted in response;
- What you did to make yourself feel better.

7. Take Control

Stress can be triggered by a problem that may on the surface seem impossible to solve. Learning how to find solutions to your problems will help you feel more in control thereby lowering your level of stress.

One problem-solving technique involves writing down the problem and coming up with as many possible solutions as you can. Decide on the good and bad points of each one and select the best solution. In detail, write down each step that you need to take as part of the solution.

8. Manage Your Time

At times, we all feel overburdened by our 'To Do' list and this is a common cause of stress. Start to prioritise your tasks by making a list of all the things that you need to do and list them in order of genuine priority.

By editing what might have started out as an overwhelming and unmanageable task list, you can break it down into a series of smaller, more manageable tasks. These can be spread out over a longer time frame, with some tasks removed from the list entirely through delegation. Identify your best time of day (you may be a morning person or an evening person) and do the important tasks that need the most energy and concentration at that time.

9. Learn to Say 'No.'

A common cause of stress is having too much to do and too little time in which to do it. Learning to say 'no' to additional or unimportant requests will help to reduce your level of stress, and may also help you develop more self-confidence.

Why do some people find it difficult to say 'no'? Remember that these barriers to saying 'no' are all self-created. You might feel reluctant to respond to a request with a straight 'no' at first. So instead practise saying phrases such as, 'I am sorry, but I can't commit to this as I have other priorities at the moment,' and, 'now is not a good time as I'm in the middle of something.'

10. Rest If You Are Ill

If you are feeling unwell, do not feel that you have to carry on regardless. A short spell of rest will enable the body to recover faster.

11. Act Positively

Make time for your friends. Talking to them about your day and the things you find difficult can help you keep things in perspective. Smiling and laughing with them will also produce hormones which help you to relax.

At the end of each day, sit back and reflect on what you've achieved, rather than spending time worrying about what still needs to be done. Try to get away every so often, if you can, even if it's only for a day out.

Develop an absorbing hobby or interest – an activity that uses your brain in a completely different way from your everyday work can be a great release. It can also be a great way to make new friends.

12. Try to accept things you can't change

It isn't always possible to change the things you don't like or find difficult, but you can try and change your own attitude to them. This way you don't build up feelings of resentment or start taking your feelings out on others.

Final Thoughts

Stress does not have to be a debilitating part of life. Successful stress management is all about learning how and when to take control. It's important to remember that you control how stress affects you. You can control the stress or let stress control you – so relax.

"When everything seems to be going against you, remember that the airplane takes off against the wind, not with it."

Henry Ford

Your Inner Chimp

The part of the brain that runs on emotions and gut instincts, makes snap judgements, and thinks in black and white

Chapter 9

Your Inner Chimp

The part of the brain that runs on emotions and gut instincts, makes snap judgements, and thinks in black and white

Introduction

Have there been times in your life when you:

- Say things thoughtlessly in the heat of the moment and regret it later?
- Wonder why you sometimes seem to be a different person from the one you want to be?
- Try to diet, but can't stop eating even though you want to?
- Really want to get fit but then quickly give up?
- Lose your temper while driving when someone cuts you up?

How often does something wind you up to the extent that you fly into a rage, ranting and raving for a few minutes, and then leaves you wondering where on earth it all came from?

According to Consultant Psychiatrist, Dr Steve Peters, these things happen because your 'Inner Chimp' is out of control. Dr Peters developed a mind management model in which he attempts to explain the neuroscience behind our behaviours in simple, easily accessible terms. He is the author of a book called "The Chimp Paradox" in which he argues there are three elements to the psychological mind.

He labels these 'The Human' ('the ego'), 'The Chimp' ('the id') and 'The Computer' ('the super-ego'). The Chimp Model explains how the mind can be seen as three teams all working for the benefit, protection and survival of the human being, but each with their own location and agenda:

- The Human (you), is mainly based in the frontal lobe, and is associated with logical thinking. It works with facts and truth.
- The Chimp, mainly based in the limbic system, is an independent emotional thinking machine. It works with feelings and impressions and acts without your permission.
- The Human and Chimp are two separate thinking machines that independently interpret our experiences in very different ways. They can work together, but either of them can take control.
- The Computer is spread throughout the brain and is a storage area for programmed thoughts and behaviours you input into it.

The Human and the Chimp can both input information into the Computer and the important thing is to store helpful information on the Computer. In this model, everyone has an inner Chimp. It thinks independently from you and it is not good or bad – It is just a Chimp.

"Whenever you have feelings, thoughts or behaviours that you do not want or welcome, then you are being hijacked by your Chimp."

Dr Steve Peters

1. The Chimp

- The Chimp is the primitive part of the brain that cannot control its impulses.
- It is the area of the mind that is driven by impressions, emotional thinking and gut instincts.
- The Chimp quickly jumps to conclusions.
- It thinks in black and white terms and can get things

completely out of perspective.
- The Chimp can be paranoid and its behaviour can be emotive, irrational and catastrophic.
- It is the root cause of anger, fear, paranoia and despair.
- Its primary motivator is survival and it goes back to a very primitive and essential part of our human development.
- When under threat, Chimps use one of the 'fight, flight or freeze' responses.
- It thinks independently from the Human mind.
- It offers emotion-based responses to situations which can be either constructive or destructive.
- It is not seen as 'good' or 'bad', it is just your inner Chimp.
- Although it can at times help you, it is often the main cause of anxiety and panic attacks.
- It acts at four times the speed of the Human.

2. The Human

- The Human part of the brain is our rational, conscious mind.
- Its functioning is evidence-based and works with facts.
- It operates a balanced judgement using logical thinking.
- It analyses factual data to establish the truth.
- It is driven by self-fulfilment – it wants satisfaction in life and to help others.
- It thinks in shades of grey rather than black and white.
- It enables you to work out puzzles, problems and to think through tricky decisions.
- It represents who you really are – what you believe is right or wrong, and what is important in your life.

3. The Computer

- The Computer is our subconscious brain.
- It is the storage area for thoughts and behaviours that you input into it.
- It starts life as an empty hard drive and collects our

experiences along the way.

- This information is stored by either the Human or the Chimp element.
- It then serves as an automatic reference point for each to access when called upon.
- The Computer operates at five times the speed of the Chimp and 20 times the speed of the Human.
- The values and beliefs stored within the computer can be positive or negative.
- Values are important as they will be a guide to the Chimp.
- The computer is only as good as the information it contains.
- Our stored beliefs can be positive, negative; some deeply hard-wired and hard to change, and some are easier to reprogram.

"I've missed more than 9,000 shots in my career. I've lost almost 300 games. 26 times I've been trusted to take the game-winning shot and missed. I've failed over and over and over again in my life. And that is why I succeed."

Michael Jordan

Story

About 30 years ago, before I learned all the techniques I now possess regarding managing my Chimp, I was working for a radio station and my Chimp was very much in control of my actions and reactions.

I remember a couple of occasions in Newcastle where I was working in a sales team for a radio station. I literally got out of my car and squared up to someone who had cut in front of me – this happened twice!

On both occasions, it didn't lead to an actual fight, but we were standing toe to toe shouting at each other with a full fist fight only one swear word away. As I think back to these incidents, it makes me both laugh and cringe as I realise how ridiculous we must have looked to all the people watching this scene unfold. It could have come directly from a Fawlty Towers – how ridiculous.

Yet at the time I couldn't do a thing about it. The 'Red Mist' came down and I was out of the car like a shot. It was only when I had got back in the car and calmed down that I realised how stupid that was and felt really ashamed of my actions. I now understand that it was in the car when it was all over that the Chimp went back to sleep and the Human was back in control, in shock as to what had just happened.

With this new understanding, I have now developed great techniques to stop the Chimp taking over as it used to. It was quite simply the Chimp responding to the aggression of the other driver with aggression – Tit for Tat. It seemed like the obvious thing for the Chimp to do, so all the chemicals kicked off in my body and the adrenaline pumped through my muscles and I was off.

You will see this very clearly on the football field when a normally calm player will suddenly lunge with a double footed tackle, or even fight with a player. The term 'Red Mist' is used for this but it should be termed 'Chimp Mist'. It is irrational, but because the Chimp is faster and stronger than the Human, it wins every time a sudden situation occurs – unless you put autopilots in place.

When I came across the Chimp Paradox I had already created an autopilot for the computer because I didn't want to lose my temper anymore. This was especially important now that I was with Julie who is a kind and gentle lady. Without knowing about the Chimp Paradox, I decided to repeat a phrase over and over until it became ingrained in my subconscious.

*The phrase I created was, 'sh*t happens and here it is.' Without really knowing what I was doing, I was creating an autopilot in my computer which basically said that bad things will happen every day so get ready for them. So when I was cut up the next time in my car by another driver my initial reaction for a split second was to hit the horn. But this time, that feeling instantly passed and the phrase came into my head, 'sh*t happens and here it is.'*

*The first time this happened I was really surprised and thought maybe it was a one off, but then it happened again and again and again – so much so that over the past two years I have only lost my temper very slightly once! This control is on-going, both when by myself and in front of people. This includes my laptop freezing on dozens of occasions, and countless incidents in the car where the old me would have gone mad. The list is endless and each time the Chimp checks with the Computer and gets the same answer: 'S**t happens and here it is.' So it goes back to sleep.*

This is extremely liberating and I recommend this highly. People say I'm a nice chap, but I used to have this snap temper where I would be fine for a long time, then I would blow like a volcano – not anymore!

"The battles that count aren't the ones for gold medals. The struggles within yourself – the invisible battles inside all of us – that's where it's at."

Jesse Owens

How Does it Work?

Dr Peters suggests that our personalities are formed by a combination of the Chimp, the Human and the Computer.

As you interact in the world or think new thoughts, both the Human and the Chimp receive and interpret this information. How you are going to react and therefore ultimately feel about that information will depend on which part of the brain you use to do the interpreting. Your Inner Chimp is often in defence or attack mode and uses emotional thinking without the use of logic and reason.

It can tend to be unrealistic and negative, making assumptions and using thoughts that are likely to be based on worry and fear, which can lead to feelings of anxiety. The Human, on the other hand, will first look for the facts of the situation before making an assessment and decision on how to think or act further. When you are in Human mode, you are more likely to think more positive and realistic thoughts, and this in turn makes you feel better.

The Chimp is more powerful and so can take control of your actions, making you irrational and out of control in a way which you regret afterwards. According to Dr Peters, your Inner Chimp has five times your Human strength. The Human may try to take back control from the Chimp, but the Chimp is much quicker and stronger and you may not succeed. For example, if you suffer from a panic attack brought on by claustrophobia, you may logically know that the situation is not dangerous but you cannot control your reaction.

Learning to recognise the difference between yourself and your Chimp is an important part of working with your mind. Whenever you have emotions or thoughts that you don't want, your Chimp is hijacking you – for example, if you:

- Have unwelcome thoughts and feelings
- Struggle to live life the way you want to
- Sabotage your own happiness and success
- Act impulsively and regret it later
- Procrastinate or can't stick to resolutions.

The Chimp will always be there. You cannot get rid of it, but you can use your Human mind to make sure it works for you and not against you.

To manage stress and impulsive reactions, we need to develop ways to stop the Chimp taking over. Dr Peters suggests the 'autopilot' – this includes recognising that the Chimp is reacting, slowing down and thinking so the Human can step in, gaining perspective and reflecting. This must kick in before the Chimp has time to act.

Much of the Chimp Paradox book is about self-awareness, and it helped me understand why I behave in certain ways. But addressing our Chimps and actually managing them is much harder. Using your newly balanced Chimp/Human to achieve success and happiness is a lifelong project.

As well as being your worst enemy at times, the Chimp can also be your best friend, and there's the paradox. There is a time and a place for everyone's Inner Chimp to prove both useful and necessary.

The Chimp thinks that the world is full of danger and that everything and everyone is a threat. His main purpose is to protect you, and his main instinct is survival. When stress hits, in whatever form, the Chimp will always react first. It isn't possible to stop this and in some instances it could actually save your life. So the first reaction you will get will always be a Chimp one, which is normal and healthy – although it is not always helpful.

You cannot bypass the Chimp part of your nature, nor can you control it with willpower. You need to acknowledge it and work through it. Although you are not responsible for the nature of your Chimp, you are responsible for managing it and ensuring it doesn't cause chaos. The key is to develop a strategy to stop the Chimp from taking over.

Summary

- There are three elements to the psychological mind – the Chimp, the Human, and the Computer.
- All three are working for the benefit, protection and survival of the human being, but each with their own agenda.
- The Human is based in the frontal lobe and is associated with logical thinking.
- The Chimp, based in the limbic system, is an independent emotional thinking machine.
- The Computer is spread throughout the brain and is storage for programmed thoughts and behaviours.
- The Human and Chimp independently interpret experiences in very different ways.
- They can both input information into the Computer.
- The important thing is to store helpful information on the Computer to affect behaviour.
- Our personalities are formed by a combination of the Chimp, the Human and the Computer.
- The Chimp can be your worst enemy at times, but can also be your best friend.
- The need is to learn to recognise the difference between yourself and your Chimp.
- The Chimp cannot be bypassed or controlled by willpower.
- It must be acknowledged and managed to prevent it taking over.
- The Chimp always checks with the computer when it's faced with a new stimulus.
- If it receives positive feedback, then it will go to sleep, if

not, it will panic.

- We need to set an autopilot on the Computer to send a positive message to the Chimp to override the natural response of the Chimp.
- An autopilot prepares the Computer to feedback a response to the Chimp that the Human wants.

Action Plan

1. The first step to managing your Chimp is to recognise that it is the Chimp reacting, not the Human.
2. Then, slow down and get perspective. This allows your Human to catch up with the situation and bring some logical, rational thinking into it.
3. Mind Management is about accepting what we feel and then managing those feelings rather than trying to change or control them.
4. Nurture your Chimp by exercising your feelings in a safe environment. This could be privately or with a non-judgemental friend. Afterwards, you will have more space to listen to the logical human side.
5. Use your Human side to talk to the Chimp with truth and logic. You can agree with your chimp but point out the alternatives. For example, you have to do a public talk at work and your inner Chimp is making your feel very anxious. Ask your Chimp, 'what is the alternative if I don't do it?' You are training your Chimp brain to listen to your Human rules.
6. It is at this point where you can create an autopilot so that the Computer feeds back to the chimp in a more positive way when faced with the public talk.
7. The Inner Voice is very powerful and can work either negatively or positively. So, when faced with a public talk, use the positive phrases described in the Inner Voice chapter on page six and repeat many times over until it becomes an auto pilot for the computer.

8. The key to dealing with your Chimp is to tidy up the Computer and establish your truths and values. You need to have a grasp of your own 'truths of life', as well as the values by which you want to live your life. For example, don't expect all people to be nice if one of your truths is that 'not all people are nice'.
9. To achieve success requires the definition of what it is you want to achieve and why. Ask yourself the question "Why can't I do what I want to do?"

Final Thoughts

The Chimp is the primitive part of the brain that cannot control its impulses. It reacts quickly in times of stress, overriding our rational Human mind, and can often get us into trouble. But its aim is to work on our behalf, by saving us from real or imagined dangers.

We need to learn to manage the Chimp so that it works in conjunction with the Human. This can be achieved by creating an autopilot feed for the Computer to send a positive message to the Chimp and make it go back to sleep when it gets woken up unnecessarily!

"It's up to you today to start making healthy choices. Not choices that are just healthy for your body, but healthy for your mind."

Steve Maraboli

Reframing

Reframing is a way of viewing and experiencing events, ideas, concepts and emotions to find more positive alternatives

Chapter 10

Reframing

Reframing is a way of viewing and experiencing events, ideas, concepts and emotions to find more positive alternatives

Introduction

Life was difficult when I was young, but this was a good thing. That experience taught me a valuable lesson that I have used ever since. I learned that you can decide how you will be affected by events; that you do not have to be a victim of circumstance, but you can choose to use the situation instead. I accidentally learned the art of Reframing.

In reframing, you choose what an event means to you. When things go wrong, you search for what is good about the situation and give that the most attention.

Some Examples:

- You had planned a day out with a friend who has cancelled at the last minute. Instead of being frustrated by the situation, you do other things: catch up on phone calls, emails, or just relax and take time for yourself.
- You're stuck in a traffic jam and are going to be late for an appointment. Instead of worrying and getting angry, use the situation to your advantage. Relax and listen to the radio, plan how you will catch up on things over the course of the day or mentally rehearse for the forthcoming event.
- A close relationship ends, which can make you feel sorry for yourself or angry with the other person. Or you could choose to use the opportunity to make a new start, to become healthier, or to just focus on yourself.

The aim of reframing is to shift your perspective to be more empowered to act, particularly if you feel stuck. Many times, merely reframing your perspective on a situation can help you change how you feel about the situation as well. A reframe needs to be felt; the new frame needs to be more emotionally compelling than the old one if it is to be accepted.

"Success is going from failure to failure with no loss of enthusiasm."

Winston Churchill

Viktor Emil Frankl the famous neurologist, psychiatrist and Holocaust survivor gave this excellent example of reframing:

Story

Once, an elderly general practitioner consulted me because of his severe depression. He could not overcome the loss of his wife who had died two years before and whom he had loved above all else.

Now how could I help him? What should I tell him? I refrained from telling him anything, but instead confronted him with a question, 'what would have happened, Doctor, if you had died first, and your wife would have had to survive you?' 'Oh,' he said, 'for her this would have been terrible; how she would have suffered!'

Whereupon I replied, 'you see, Doctor, such a suffering has been spared her, and it is you who have spared her this suffering – to be sure at the price that you have now to survive and mourn her.' He said no word but shook my hand and calmly left the office. In some way, suffering ceases to be suffering at the moment it finds a meaning, such as the meaning of a sacrifice.

Many fields regularly use reframing, including therapy, coaching and even marketing and sales. Techniques of reframing can also be used to cultivate critical thinking and creative skills. The inventor of Velcro noticed how difficult it was to get burrs out of his clothing and decided this could be useful for attaching things together. He reframed the situation and used it creatively.

"Wise people learn not to dread but actually to welcome problems."

M. Scott Peck

In life you will get problems – that's accepted. You will be better at facing them, solving them, becoming less depressed and upset if you learn to embrace the challenge. It is unlikely that many people would welcome problems, but we can learn to do so by getting in the habit of seeing problems as 'opportunities in disguise'. We can learn to welcome problems by deliberately trying to see what's good about them.

I personally use this technique on a daily basis whenever I am faced with negative situations. This helps me greatly to keep a positive mindset most of the day thereby bringing more positive things into my life.

Story

I was working for an advertising agency and I was informed that I would be made redundant in the near future. This was initially a shock, but as I processed this, I discovered that this would actually give me the opportunity to finally achieve one of my dreams, which was to run my own successful business. I had been employed for most of my life, apart from a two-year period where I ran my own business that subsequently failed.

The great thing about a failure is that, if you learn from it, then it's not a failure but a learning experience, and that is exactly what happened to me. I learned a great deal about how not to run a business, so this time round I am not making the same mistakes and the business is growing nicely.

During my time at this agency, I had two outstanding years where I was the top performer in the company, bringing in record amounts of revenue. On the back of this I could have comfortably been successful in securing a position with another agency following redundancy, but because of my re-frame I realised that there was a better option. I chose instead to let the redundancy materialise and use the money to set up my own business – and JD Mindcoach Ltd was born.

The reframing changed my belief system in what could be achieved and kept me thinking positively, which allowed me to create a picture in my head of the kind of business I would like to run. As I kept reframing (every time something negative came into my thoughts) I found that the possibility of running a successful business became more and more possible.

I now sit here writing my first book while running a successful business with great potential across many areas. It is very exciting to see the way the business is developing and it was down to my reframing of the redundancy situation which gave me the confidence to take the brave step. I left employed work and entered the scary but thrilling world of self-employment.

"A person who never made a mistake, never tried anything new."

Albert Einstein

Benefits of Reframing

I believe that in every negative situation there is a seed of positivity, which is of equal or greater benefit. It will help to use any trick you can to think of problems as 'good'. There was a business executive who would always respond to bad news with an enthusiastic, "that's good!" and then he would look for ways of making what happened turn out for the best. It might sound crazy, but his was a practical response to something that had already happened. He was very successful, and an important part of his success was doubtless due to his response to problems.

Attitudes like that mean that you don't hide away from problems and you keep your eyes open while dealing with them. The strange thing is that after doing this a few times you will have confidence that you really mean it, and will eventually be glad it happened.

Sales trainers often give their salespeople mental tricks to help them see rejections as not so bad, or even as a good thing. Let's say you are selling something door-to-door, and someone slams a door in your face. How could you possibly see that as a good thing? Salespeople who succeed learn to think of ideas as to how a rejection could be a good thing. Although at first those ideas might not make a salesperson feel any better and the thoughts themselves would seem unnatural and unfamiliar, eventually it becomes as natural and familiar as the old way of thinking and they no longer feel bad when people say no. They might even feel good.

One of the classic reframes of rejection used by salespeople the world over is:

'This is a numbers game. If my sales record shows that one out of every 10 people say yes, then that means the person who said no brought me closer to the one who will say yes!'

It's all in the perspective. Reframing seems like something superficial, but it is a tremendously powerful tool. People who accomplish things in this world all learn to do it, consciously or not.

"Challenges are what make life interesting and overcoming them is what makes life meaningful."

Joshua J. Marine

I experienced a situation in my basketball career where I needed to reframe in a big way – to not only keep myself sane but also on track. The following situation was a tough one to face.

Story

When I was 25 years of age, I was playing for England and semi-professionally for Team Fiat in Coventry. It was an exciting time; I had played all over Europe and America, and life was good. It was then that I received a call that changed my life. It was a call from the basketball manager of Sunderland Basketball club, who said he would like to come and meet with me for a chat.

That chat turned out to be the offer of a professional playing contract – playing the sport I loved, full time! As you can imagine, it didn't take me long to agree to this and I moved from Nottingham to Sunderland. I was housed with a couple of Americans and had my own company car with my name on the side! Life didn't get much better than this – until about six weeks into training when things suddenly and dramatically changed.

I'd spent time weight training with these big American players and was trying to keep up with them when I felt an increasing pain in my back. I ignored it until I was playing an exhibition match back in Nottingham, slipped on a wet patch and popped a disc in my back. The technical term is a prolapsed disc, but most people refer to it as a slipped disc.

I went into the hospital and was on traction to stretch my back out and being prepared for an operation. The directors from the club came to see me and sent me to a famous Osteopath, who worked on my back and got me running again. I knew then that I wouldn't last long in the game because I was in a fair bit of pain. I had a decision to make.

Do I carry on playing for Sunderland, knowing it would possibly be short-term, or do I go back to my safe old job? I had made a commitment to playing professionally for Sunderland so I carried on.

I ended up playing for another two years all over Europe and my final game was winning the biggest competition in basketball – the Playoff Final at Empire Pool Wembley, 1981. There was a sell-out crowd of 10,000 people and live BBC TV coverage. What a way to finish!

As you can imagine, I went through a great deal of negative inner voice dialogue about my situation and I had to work very hard to reframe this thinking. But with persistence I developed a habit that let me see the positive things in every negative situation, and this is still with me to this day.

There are a few principles to keep in mind when considering the reframing technique. A reframe is far more effective when you understand what's going on behind the thought:

1. **Events or situations do not have inherent meaning.** Even when something seemingly terrible happens, it is

only terrible because of the way you look at it. This is not trivialising the event – you can be sad when something seemingly bad occurs, but even a 'bad' event can be given a 'good' meaning.

2. **Every thought has a hidden 'frame' behind it.** The frame is your underlying beliefs and assumptions that are implied by your thought. For example, when you think you'll never get that promotion because the boss doesn't like you – the frame is 'the boss doesn't like me'.

3. **There is a positive intention behind every negative thought.** Your inner voice expressing negativity is only doing so because it wants to help you in some way. By finding the positive intentions behind your thoughts, you can work with your mind to find a positive reframe.

At its simplest, reframing involves just two steps: observing a negative thought, and then replacing it with a positive one.

There are three main types of negative thoughts that it is most helpful to reframe:-

1. **Limiting beliefs.** A limiting belief is a thought that prevents you from accepting your full potential. The consequences of accepting your limiting beliefs rather than challenging them mean you end up not achieving what you want.

   You can counter a limiting belief by reframing thoughts based on it, and so reduce the chance of it getting in the way of your goals. For example, 'I'm not good enough,' becomes, 'I've faced many challenges before, and I've conquered all of them. Also, they rarely turn out to be anything significant in the grand scheme of things.'

'People never listen to me,' becomes, 'while it's unfortunate that this person doesn't appreciate my idea as much as they should, many other people do.'

2. **When you wish that something acceptable were better.** Have you ever had a really enjoyable night staying in, but felt like you missed out the next day when you heard about something exciting your friends had done? We tend to beat ourselves up in these kinds of situations, even though we had a good time.

   Rather than letting your mind be filled with negative thoughts, take advantage of this easy reframing situation and enjoy the moment even more: 'I am pleased that my friends had a good time, but I am glad that I stayed in because I had a really enjoyable night pampering, relaxing and eating chocolate.'

3. **Specific problem areas.** This can often be related to limiting beliefs. Perhaps you are working on a specific area of your life, such as wanting to lose weight. You want to go to the gym, but it's raining and you don't want to get wet. In this situation, you can use reframing as a way to motivate yourself to go: 'It is raining and I'll get wet on the way to the gym, but it is worth it for the sense of achievement and the great hot showers afterwards.'

Summary

- Reframing means changing your perspective on a given situation to give it a more positive meaning.
- A reframe needs to have an emotional impact to be accepted.
- Reframing can be used to help remove limiting beliefs.
- Reframing can help us to appreciate positive moments we might otherwise miss.
- Our assumptions make us give meaning to events that don't have any inherent meaning.
- Even when the inner voice says something negative, there

is positive intention behind it.

- The first step in reframing is to observe your negative thoughts.
- The second step is to replace the negative thoughts with a more positive one.
- There are common negative thought patterns, and you can arm yourself against them in advance.

Action Plan

Here are some valuable tactics to help you reframe, by replacing your negative thoughts with positive ones:

1. **Use a thought journal**
   Anytime you have a negative thought, write it down in your journal – you will be surprised at what you learn about yourself by doing this regularly. Keep a small notepad in your pocket or bag so it is available at all times.

2. **Wear a rubber wristband**
   Wear a band around your wrist, which should be tight enough that it stays on and can make a nice snap when pulled. Anytime you have a negative thought, give the rubber band a snap. This is one of the fastest ways to stop the negative thought in its tracks and change behaviour, although it may feel a little ridiculous initially.

3. **Use milder wording**
   You should start doing this immediately. Words do matter, and if your thought is expressed using a milder negative, you won't feel as bad. For example, if you were to think, 'I really hate that person,' you feel worse than if you thought, 'I don't like that person.'

4. **Ask yourself: 'What is the best way for me to accomplish this?'**
   The phrase 'best way' implies that there are multiple ways around the problem and focuses on the positive when you are facing a challenge or fear.

5. **Ask yourself: 'What can I learn from this?'**
   Now, instead of having a problem, you have a way to improve yourself. Every challenge is also an opportunity to learn, so take advantage of it.

6. **Challenge your assumptions**
   Try to work out what the frame behind your thought is – It is likely that you have a limiting belief that is encouraging you to think negatively about your situation. Finding reasons why they aren't true enables you to chip away at the beliefs causing the negative thoughts. This is the most powerful long-term reframing technique, and it is far more effective if you've been keeping a thought journal.

Final Thoughts

Reframing is seeing the current situation from a different perspective, which can be tremendously helpful in decision making, problem-solving, and learning. We know that we will encounter many problems in life, and the aim is not to get beaten down by them.

Every negative situation has a positive side if we only know how to look for it. Problems should be viewed as 'opportunities in disguise' – using reframing techniques allows you to do that.

There seems to be wisdom in the old adage, 'every cloud has a silver lining,', so go out and start looking for it today.

"I have not failed. I've just found 10,000 ways that don't work."

Thomas Alva Edison

Your Belief System

The mental system consisting of interrelated items of assumptions, beliefs, ideas, and knowledge that an individual holds about anything

Chapter 11

Your Belief System - is it real?

The mental system consisting of interrelated items of assumptions, beliefs, ideas, and knowledge that an individual holds about anything

Introduction

Belief systems are very powerful and dictate many of the decisions and actions we take. A belief system you hold may be real to you, but it may not actually be real. Because you believe it and it seems real, this means it becomes your reality and you act as if it is real.

The mind is an amazing thing and each year scientists are discovering new and fascinating things about this miracle of nature. The following information describes surprising facts about the brain and maybe indicates how our thinking processes and belief systems can affect our bodies so much.

"Believe you can and you're halfway there."

Theodore Roosevelt

The Science of the Brain

Researchers at the Stanford University School of Medicine have spent the past few years engineering a new imaging model, which they call 'array tomography'. In conjunction with novel computational software, they stitch together image slices into a three-dimensional image that can be rotated, penetrated and navigated.

They found that the brain's complexity is beyond anything they'd imagined. 'Almost to the point of being beyond belief,' says Stephen Smith, a Professor of molecular and cellular physiology, and senior author of the paper describing the study.

A typical, healthy brain houses some 200 billion nerve cells, which are connected to one another via hundreds of trillions of synapses. Each synapse functions like a microprocessor, and tens of thousands of them can connect a single neuron to other nerve cells. In the cerebral cortex alone, there are roughly 125 trillion synapses, which is about how many stars fill 1,500 Milky Way galaxies.

These synapses are, of course, so tiny (less than a thousandth of a millimetre in diameter) that humans have not been able to see with great clarity what exactly they do and how, apart from knowing that their numbers vary over time. That is, until now.

One synapse, by itself, is more like a microprocessor than a mere on/off switch – with both memory storage and information processing elements. In fact, one synapse may contain around 1,000 molecular-scale switches. A single human brain has more switches than all the computers and routers and Internet connections on Earth!

Smith adds that this gives us a glimpse into brain tissue at a level of detail never before attained: 'The entire anatomical context of the synapses is preserved. You know right where each one is, and what kind it is.'

These facts about the brain really underline the power of the mind and how we can use it to our advantage, according to our current understanding. We also know that as the years go by and our ability to investigate deeper will reveal even more staggering facts about our mind that will make today's stunning revelations appear ordinary by comparison.

"You become what you believe."

Oprah Winfrey

Story

Difficulty getting to sleep can sometimes be attributed to a belief system you have developed over time. A belief system may tell you that, 'you always have trouble getting to sleep,' or, 'if you wake up you can't get back to sleep.'

I used to believe that if I came in from a networking event or a party late at night I would have to get a drink of milk, watch TV and unwind for about an hour before I could go to bed. If I didn't I would be too 'wide awake' to fall asleep. Sure enough, every time I came in from an evening event I was convinced that I was 'too wired' to go straight to sleep. So I would go through my 'tried and tested' routine and, lo and behold, I would be asleep within a couple of minutes.

About two years ago I created a new rule where the TV would be switched off at 9PM and I could read or listen to my radio instead. Not long after this new rule was in place, I came home late one evening and was about to put the TV on but realised that I couldn't switch it on. I didn't fancy listening to the radio or reading, so I went to bed and amazingly I was asleep within a couple of minutes.

This really surprised me and since then I go straight to bed when I get in, and fall asleep straight away. I now have a new belief system that tells me I can go straight to bed when I get in late from an event. This new belief system is in place because I believe it's true, so it works.

I wonder what belief systems you have in place which are real to you but are not, in fact, real.

What is a Belief System?

We all have belief systems that are personal to us and have been developed by all the experiences we have been through up to this point in our lives. You may have a fear of speaking, or believe that people you meet don't like you, or you think that you can't get back to sleep when you wake in the night.

Some of the great minds of the past gave us great insight into the power of the mind:

"Whether you think you can or can't, either way you are right."

Henry Ford

Jonathan Wells put it so well when he described how our personal belief systems are developed:

"Our personal beliefs play a huge role in how we view our own life. Your estimation of your successes and failures will depend entirely on the framework of your personal beliefs. Our beliefs provide a structured process through which we evaluate everything in our lives."

We develop our personal beliefs about reality, based on how we interpret the world around us, according to our observations and experiences. There are two major aspects that contribute to our personal beliefs: an emotional component and a logical component.

1. **Beliefs are the blending of logic and emotions.**
   In some cases, a belief starts out mainly as a theory; assumptions are made based on logical observations and deductions. In other cases, a new belief grows out of an

emotional viewpoint that seems to be supported by logic.

It's the blending of these two major components that forms the basic structure of our personal beliefs. We use them to try to make sense of the things going on around us and to form assumptions about probable future results.

2. **Beliefs are accepted as facts.**
   Once established, beliefs are accepted as fact and are rarely subject to scrutiny. Much like the operating system on your computer, they become our 'personal operating system'; our beliefs control how we sort and file every bit of input data. Everything we see, experience, think and feel is adjusted to fit with our beliefs. In other words, our version of reality is a creation of our beliefs.

3. **Change Your Beliefs – Change Your Reality.**
   George Orwell once said that, 'myths which are believed tend to become true.' This is especially true on an individual basis. By now, most of us realise that our perception of reality is heavily influenced by our beliefs, but the full extent of this influence is often underestimated. Each of us has a variety of methods for altering our reality so it conforms to what we believe to be real.

   From the moment we were born, our subconscious mind has been busy collecting and processing information. Combined with our experiences, this information is used to create our beliefs about who we are as a person, and how we fit into the world around us.

Because these beliefs are based on our evaluations and also on the emotional conclusions of our personal experiences, they are accepted by your subconscious as being absolutely true. Your subconscious mind then uses these personal 'truths' to construct your personal version of the real world. In other words, your beliefs become the foundation of your internal map of reality.

"The only person you are destined to become is the person you decide to be."

Ralph Waldo Emerson

Story

When I was young, I remember several events which caused me anxiety, and because of this, I didn't perform well. One was when I was in a workshop with about 20 people around a boardroom style table. We had to introduce ourselves to the group and I remember very well my anxiety building up as each person introduced themselves and shared what they did for a living. As the number of people in front of me became fewer and fewer, I could feel the pressure growing.

I could feel my heart beating faster, my palms sweating, the voice in my head being very negative and just wanting to simply die on the spot. As the person before me was finishing, I was screaming inside and was petrified. As I opened my mouth to speak, my voice was shaking and so was my body. I managed to stumble through my name in a trembling voice and I was so embarrassed. I believed that I would be nervous and I was.

To the mind, your map is a reality.

The way in which your map is constructed will determine many aspects of your life. It will be a major determining factor in your success or failure, your happiness or unhappiness, and your satisfaction or dissatisfaction with your entire life experience.

Remember when people believed that the world was flat? That

belief completely altered the way they viewed and interacted with their reality. It didn't matter that the world was really round. They believed it was flat and that belief had a powerful influence on their version of the real world. It changed the way they interpreted the facts.

We customise the facts to fit our map.

We interpret the facts in a way that allows them to support our internal map of reality. If we have created a map where opportunity is everywhere, that's what we will see. When our map is based on opportunity, we won't view challenges as obstacles because that wouldn't harmonise with our map.

Here's the catch. For most people, the way the map creates their reality on a day-to-day basis is completely outside of their conscious awareness. And because the process takes place on a subconscious level, they don't see how they are creating their own reality. Instead of feeling like something they created, it seems like it's coming from an external source. The map is not reality!

We also create an emotional attachment to our map. It's our personal version of what is real and we have a vested interest in verifying its accuracy. We want it to be real because it's familiar, and that makes us feel safe and secure. This is why we are willing to distort, or even ignore, almost anything that might undermine our map.

Despite our best efforts though, sometimes our map of reality becomes unravelled. Usually, this involves emotionally charged events that don't fit the map and can't be ignored, and this changes our reality.

New beliefs are the key to a better map.

For personal growth to occur, the map needs to be redrawn from time to time. This can be scary as it can feel as though our life is imploding until we realise that we are not the map; we create the map based on past beliefs which can be changed.

Updating our beliefs automatically changes our map. This is how we create a more pleasing version. When we systematically dismantle our limiting beliefs, and replace them with empowering beliefs, the topography of our map will conform.

When we replace self-doubt with self-confidence, fear with curiosity, or pessimism with optimism, our map will rearrange itself to support those beliefs. The world around us will look and feel different, and we will be more comfortable with our place in it. We will have created a better internal map of reality.

Story

A few days before writing this chapter, the leader of the Green Party was being quizzed on television about specific facts and figures and she was collapsing in a heap. As I watched her reaction, I could empathise with her and could see exactly what she was going through. Her inner voice was too negative, she wasn't relaxed and was collapsing under the pressure of the questions she was being asked. Because her inner voice was now so negative it was inevitable that she would not recover from this.

It was a PR disaster for this poor lady and she tried to explain that this was one of 'those things which happen from time to time' to everyone. But there was something else going on here – her belief system allowed her to anchor back to insecurities she will have experienced in her earlier life, which resulted in this collapse on TV. She is clearly a good communicator and a confident person to be elected the leader of the Green Party. However, it just shows that when under pressure without a positive belief system, disaster can hit anyone at any time.

Summary

- Our personal beliefs play a huge role in how we view life.
- Our perception of reality is heavily influenced by our beliefs.
- Beliefs are the blending of logic and emotions.
- Once established, beliefs are accepted as fact and are rarely subject to scrutiny.
- Your beliefs become the foundation of your internal map of reality.
- To the mind, your map is a reality.
- We customize the facts to fit our map.
- The map is not reality.
- New beliefs are the key to a better map.
- Challenge your beliefs to create new better beliefs.

Action Plan

1. Take a situation where you are struggling with negative emotions.
2. Think deeply about this situation and why you feel this way.
3. Write down your thoughts.
4. See if you can challenge your belief system about this.
5. Create a new belief system to add to your map of reality.
6. Repeat this over and over again until this becomes your new reality.

Final Thoughts

Belief systems are the stories we tell ourselves to define our personal sense of reality. Every human being has a belief system that they utilise, and it is through this mechanism that we individually live our daily lives. We govern our thoughts, words and actions, and 'make sense' of the world around us.

We should constantly challenge our ingrained belief systems to create a better reality for us to operate in.

"Whatever your mind can conceive and can believe, it can achieve."

Napoleon Hill

The Law of Attraction

Attracting into our lives whatever we put attention, energy and focus on, for good and for bad

Chapter 12

The Law of Attraction

Attracting into our lives whatever we put attention, energy and focus on, for good and for bad

Introduction

The Law of Attraction states that 'like attracts like'. By focusing on positive or negative thoughts, a person brings positive or negative experiences into their life because people and their thoughts are both made from pure energy. The philosophy is that energy attracts like energy.

Thoughts are forms of energy that are sent ahead and eventually manifest as physical matter. Your thoughts create your reality, including finances, relationships, health and the environment. In fact, there is no aspect of your life that is not affected by your thoughts. Thoughts have a force that is capable of rearranging people, places and events in the world around you to produce what look like coincidences, accidents and serendipity. **And the most profound truth of all is that by changing your thoughts you can change your future, and manifest whatever you want through the operation of the Law of Attraction.**

"A man is but the product of his thoughts. What he thinks he becomes."

Gandhi

Your thoughts play an important role in the manifestation process; however, your thoughts alone are not causing the attraction – It's actually your vibration. The attraction process consists of:

- Your words affecting your thoughts

- Your thoughts affecting your feelings
- Your feelings affecting your vibration
- Your vibration is what attracts things to you.

Everything in the universe is made out of energy. All energy vibrates at incredible speeds and every single thing on this earth has a different vibrational range. The vibrations are signals you send to the world, the universe gets them and sends back the exact vibrations that match the ones you have. **Your feelings are most important in this process of attraction as they will affect the vibration you send out.** That's why it's important to feel good so you can receive positive vibrations back that will match your personal broadcasting.

Monitoring your thoughts can be hard work, but monitoring your feelings is relatively simple. The better you feel, the better your energy and the more you will attract the things you want into your life.

Visualisation works.

I am now married to Julie and I visualised a happy marriage for years before I met her. I even went one step further with another technique I read about which involved a picture frame. I wrote my blog on the morning of my wedding day entitled 'I get married today!' and I share this blog with you below.

Blog

Wow, I can't believe the 18 months have gone by so quickly since I asked Julie to marry me and she said yes!

It has been a wonderful journey and we have arrived at the day of destiny where our lives are changed forever. She is a beautiful, gentle person with a heart of gold. We get on so well and I believe we are going to have a very good marriage.

As I got dressed this morning, I noticed the picture frame on my sideboard and remembered the significance of this frame. About two and a half years ago I bought an empty picture frame with the intention of visualising a wedding photo filling that frame. Every day I would stare at the picture frame and visualise myself and my bride, happy and married, on the wedding day.

Over the months, the picture started to take shape until I could see the shot of us smiling and happy. Once that had happened I didn't need to do it anymore and I let the law of attraction do the rest. I couldn't actually see her face, but I could see how tall she was and that we were stood outside in the garden of the venue where we would get married.

When I started this process there wasn't anyone in my life. I just simply believed that if I kept positive and imagined it, then one day I would meet and marry the woman of my dreams.

Something else I did about three years ago was to ask Barry, my good friend, whether he would be my best man as I was going to get married again. At the time, I had no thoughts about meeting someone but I felt something inside. He immediately said yes not realising that this would become a reality. I again kept a positive mindset and Julie was brought into my life.

Barry gave the most amazing best man's speech I have ever heard and the whole day was perfect. As I sat listening to Barry deliver his speech I remember thinking back to all the times I had visualised that picture frame. I remembered the hundreds of times I had been to his home to eat with him and his dear wife Linda, as a single man. Yet now here I was sittting and listening to a brilliant speech at my wedding!

I continue to visualise the 24 things I have on my Dream Board every day as if I have already achieved them. Things like funding an orphanage, flying in a helicopter over Victoria Falls and speaking in Dubai. When some of these things come to pass, it gives me the faith to believe that if I continue to visualise achieving these, many will become reality.

The wedding day was perfect, as were the honeymoon arrangements. I had visualised both of these events in detail going well and smoothly, and they did. I believe there is power in positive visualisation and that it really can make a difference. Of course, not everything will work out exactly as you visualise it, but I really do believe that more things will work out the way you want if you take visualisation seriously.

"We all possess more power and greater possibilities than we realise, and visualising is one of the greatest of these powers."

Genevieve Berhrend

How to Use the Law of Attraction

Spend some time each day visualising the things you want, exactly how you have decided that you want them. Do this on a daily basis, and believe 100% that by doing such things they will manifest in your life. If you expect to see results regardless of how improbable such results may be – you will see results. You are in complete control of your life and your future.

By changing your thoughts, you can change your future and manifest whatever you want through the operation of the Law of Attraction. But you also must have a burning desire for a certain outcome. You must have complete belief in the fact that it can happen and positive expectation that it will happen. Lastly, you have to take some action towards making it happen. Put simply:

Desire + Belief + Expectancy + Action = Manifestation

Manifestation simply refers to the appearance of what you want in the world. However, manifesting your desired object involves more than just goal-setting and thinking positively; to be successful it involves intense visualisation, passion and feeling.

Truly successful people live their ambition every moment of their lives – or at the very least they keep their objectives fresh in their minds every day. They work at what they do, at what they love, and at what they want. They think about what they want and they feel the joy and intensity of emotion that will come from getting it. It is this consistent mental and emotional energy that fuels the process of manifestation.

1. **Desire**

   It is important to decide what you want from any area of your life. This is the hardest part of the whole process. We are conditioned to give our attention to the things that we don't want, which is why the majority of people are not living a happy, deliberately created lifestyle. To find your desire, it can be as easy as looking at what you don't want and flipping it over.

   A simple way to identify what you want and don't want is to first list all the things you don't like about a particular area of your life, such as your finances, for example:

   <u>Things I don't like about my money</u> – I have no spare cash; I can't buy things when I want; I'm worried about my debt; I have more bills than income

   Then list the exact opposite of the negative things you

have written so that you can work out what you actually like, for example:

What I should give my attention to – I always have spare cash; I have money to buy things when I want; I feel good about my money; I have large savings accounts.

Decide what you want and then don't doubt yourself. Make sure it is something you have strong enthusiasm for. You need to figure out what you want more than anything else, no matter how impossible the goal may sound right now. It could be that you want to be a millionaire, or to get a great new job, or to be the perfect weight.
Focus on what you want rather than focusing on what is. Put your emphasis and energy on those things you want to manifest in your life.
For instance, if you want to bring a loving and fulfilling relationship into your life, avoid falling into the victim trap of 'I'm lonely'. Instead, use your imagination and focus on how you will feel when you do have a warm and loving relationship.

2. Belief

Do a little daydreaming about the big, seemingly impossible dreams. Many of us only dare to dream about the things we think are possible by most people's standards, and so we tend to be fairly limited in our requests.

Instead of dreaming about winning the lottery, we ask the universe for a raise. Why not come up with a few extraordinary dreams as well? To really harness the power of the Law of Attraction, we must realise that we have unlimited potential.

When you set a goal and put your energy into it, be aware of the resistance that comes up which is self-doubt, its source being rooted in the subconscious mind. The doubt carries a negative vibration, which is the opposite of manifesting your aspiration. Having an awareness of the doubts that crop up in your head will make it easier for you to identify what is stopping you so you can work on removing those blockages by shifting your subconscious beliefs.

So take some time and think about what it would feel like to be a millionaire, to live on a tropical island, or to change the world. Just imagine, without effort or overthinking. Manifestation is very simple – you just need to remove all doubt and go with the flow.

3. Expectation

Expect to see signs and results. Make sure you seize any opportunity that could help achieve your goal. If you are visualising well and consistently, you should be coming across an unusual amount of unanticipated events, which occurred because of your positive visualisation, meaning that you are getting closer to your goal.

For example, if you are someone who has been consistently visualising a life partner and you see a poster for a speed dating event, it is not just coincidence. But you will never get there unless you act upon serendipity, so be assertive and grasp every opportunity.

4. Action

Materialisation can only occur when you are in true alignment with your desires. Good emotions such as love, joy, happiness and contentment are signs that you are in alignment with your desires and your task is to maintain those feelings and constantly feel better. There are various ways to achieve this:

- **Meditation** – When you meditate, you release your thoughts and move into a far more relaxed state. Using this process, you are no longer resisting your desires and so your vibration begins to increase. Doing this for five to ten minutes a day can be beneficial.

- **Affirmations** – Affirmations can be very powerful when used over long periods of time. Stating positive, present-tense statements to yourself on a regular basis will help you to believe those affirmations are true.

- **Visualisation** – Giving yourself a few minutes of quiet time, where you can visualise already having your desires materialised, is invaluable. See this thing as already yours and experience the positive feelings associated with achieving your desires. Visualise every day; being consistent is one of the most important parts of the process.

  The easiest way for me to do this is to use my Dream Board every morning in my quiet time. I do this every day no matter what I have to do that day. If I have to get up at 4AM to give me the time to do this I will, as I know the impact this is having on my life.

- **Dream Board** – Creating and observing your own dream board is a great way to remind yourself of your desires and the feelings you have for them. To create a Dream Board, simply collect some images that make you feel good and create a collage about your desires. Full details of this are in Chapter 14.

- **Appreciation Journal** – This is a diary that you complete once per day, listing all of the things that you are grateful for during that day. Once you've completed a list, go over each item on your list and spend a few seconds thinking about the feelings as to why you appreciate it so much.

These are suggestions for processes to help with materialising your desires. They should only be done if they feel good to you and so maintain your positive vibrations.

"How wonderful it is that nobody need wait a single moment before starting to improve the world."

Anne Frank

Summary

- The Law of Attraction simply says that you attract into your life whatever you think about and feel.
- By focusing on positive or negative thoughts, a person brings positive or negative experiences into their life.
- Everything is made of pure energy – thoughts are forms of energy that are sent ahead and eventually create a new reality.
- By changing your thoughts, you can change your future and manifest whatever you want.
- Your words affect your thoughts, which affect your feelings, which affect the vibrations you send out.
- Vibrations are signals and the Universe sends back the exact matching vibrations.
- The better you feel, the better your energy and the more you will attract positive things into your life.
- For the Law of Attraction to work, you must have a burning desire for a certain outcome.
- You need to have complete and positive belief in the fact that it can happen.
- You also have to take some action towards making it happen.
- Methods include meditation, affirmations, visualisation, the Dream Board, and appreciation journal.
- Consistency is the key to your success.

"It's your place in the world; it's your life. Go on and do all you can with it, and make it the life you want to live."

Mae Jemison

Action Plan

1. **Relax your mind**
   Meditate for five to ten minutes every day. Just sit somewhere quiet, make yourself comfortable and close your eyes. Take three deep breaths into your nose and out of your mouth and then try to empty your mind completely for a minute before attempting to visualise.

2. **Visualise your dreams**
   Do this daily in great detail, experiencing the joyful feelings of achieving those dreams. Use a Dream Board if this method works for you, or use your imagination freely, but keep rehearsing the dreams to refine every little detail. If your mind strays during visualisation, open your eyes, shake your head, and then close your eyes and continue.

3. **Write your wish down**
   Start with, 'I am so happy and grateful now that...' and finish the sentence (or paragraph) telling the Universe what it is that you want. Write it in the present tense as if you have it right now. Every day until your wish comes true, close your eyes and imagine your desire as if it's happening right now.

4. **Feel it**
   Feel the way now that you will after receiving your wish. You must act, speak, and think as if you are receiving it now. This is actually the most important, powerful step

in using the Law of Attraction because this is where it starts working.

5. **Show gratitude**
   Write down all the things the Universe has given you. Be thankful for what you already have and be thankful for all the things that will be given you. Gratitude will draw more things into your life.

6. **Trust**
   Be patient – don't get upset if these things don't happen immediately. Just remember to be consistent in your dreaming.

7. **Stay positive**
   Be aware that the emotions you send out on a minute-by-minute basis will come back to you in direct proportion. If you want a happy life, be happy now no matter what you are going through.

Final Thoughts

Positive things come to positive people, so practise a good demeanour about life. It is important to enjoy every day and to stop using negative words that influence thoughts, feelings and ultimately the vibrations sent out into the Universe. Energy attracts like energy, so you will get back whatever you send out – you can unconsciously call bad things into your life by not focusing on the good things.

We all have limiting beliefs, fears and blocks that have become the interior landscape of our minds and cannot be changed overnight just by thinking positive thoughts. To become a master at manifesting with the law of attraction, we have to undo the patterns that have been stored in our unconscious and replace them with positive, empowering patterns.

The Law of Attraction is a fundamental universal law which states that we can change our future by changing our thoughts and feelings. Provided that we also have a burning desire, complete belief and positive expectation. Finally we must consistently take the appropriate action to achieve that future.

"Your imagination is your preview of life's coming attractions."

Albert Einstein

The Power of Visualisation

A technique involving focusing on positive mental images in order to achieve a particular goal

Chapter 13

The Power of Visualisation

A technique involving focusing on positive mental images in order to achieve a particular goal

Introduction

This is a most powerful tool that I have used and which has dramatically changed my life. I played about with this concept for many years, not knowing the power contained within this simple technique.

I remember the time when I worked for local radio station Metro Radio in Newcastle, and I first came across this concept. You will no doubt have heard of people putting a picture of something they want on a fridge and looking at it every day until they receive it. At the time, I really wanted a Jaguar car, so using this principle I found a picture of the car I wanted and put it up on my wall next to my desk.

Then, I went to a Jaguar garage and sat in a brand new Jaguar. I felt the leather of the seats and the steering wheel, and smelled the leather. I imagined that I was driving the car as I sat in it and I even told the salesman that I would be back in the near future to purchase one.

At first I looked at that picture every day, then as time went by it was every other day then every week until I stopped imagining driving that car. It won't be a surprise to you to know that the car never appeared in my life.

Technique

Now, 30 years later, I have brought this concept back into my life, but this time I am taking it much more seriously.

The difference this time is that I have taken visualisation to another level. I now get an image of what I want to achieve and look at it every day. The actual visualisation technique I use is an NLP (Neuro-Linguistic Programming) technique, which makes the whole process much more powerful. This involves using all my senses of hearing, smell, taste, and touch to bring the visualisation to life and to also feel the emotions associated with the visualisation. You won't be surprised to learn that, 30 years later, I am driving my dream Audi.

This time, I visualised driving the car every day, I saw it parked outside my house and I could even see myself driving through the Derbyshire Peak District. I had someone next to me (at that time I didn't know it would be my wife, Julie). I wouldn't let a day go by where I didn't see myself in the car and feel the feelings of owning this car. I saw myself driving from inside the car looking out, and also from the outside imagining that I was approaching it to get in and drive off.

"Limitations live only in our minds. But if we use our imaginations, our possibilities become limitless."

Jamie Paolinetti

Story

Dame Kelly Holmes is a remarkable example of the power of visualisation. She was a very good athlete who performed well but unfortunately never fulfilled her potential until the 2004 Athens Olympics. The year before the Olympics she was training hard and knew she was past her best at the age of 33 and that this was her last chance to win an Olympic gold. With just one year to go, she received severe leg injuries and she gave it all up.

With the huge pressure she faced, she took medication

and was cutting herself with a knife. It seemed like her dream was over, but she was reminded of something she had said as a 14-year-old girl, which was fundamental in the amazing turnaround she experienced to win the double gold. This is what she said: ***'Since the age of 14 I've believed that whatever barriers come my way one day I will be Olympic Champion.'***

As a youngster growing up, she visualised standing on the podium with a gold medal around her neck and the national anthem playing. She visualised this scene plus crossing the line in first place so many times that it created a pathway in her brain which was triggered when she was reminded of this. So she spent the next 12 months totally committed to winning a gold medal.

What Happens During Visualisation?

Every time we visualise, we create a pathway in the brain that gets broader the more we visualise. Chemicals are released into the brain, which create this pathway. There comes a point when the pathway is so broad that it causes us to do things subconsciously. For example, professional swimmers will get up at 4AM every day to get to the pool and swim. This takes great dedication and effort, and the ones who make it to the top are the ones who visualise themselves training and racing over and over again.

By doing this, they have created a very powerful pathway in the mind that gets them up in the morning without their conscious mind being aware of it. The subconscious takes over and they do things automatically. This is what happened to Dame Kelly Holmes, who was reminded of this commitment she had made. Because of the pathway she had created during her career, she made a decision to get back to training, no matter what pain she was in, and to start working towards the finals in 2004.

She had a year to get her times down to potential winning times and this took all five of the Mental Resilience pillars of Commitment, Motivation, Confidence, Control and Focus. She worked all day every day and dedicated her life for a full year to fulfil the dream. The pathway in her mind grew broader and broader, helping her to keep going under the most difficult of circumstances.

In an interview with the Daily Mirror on 16th September 2012, she told of the extreme pressure she was under that led to the self-harming:

'She always has a radiant smile lighting up her face – but behind it Dame Kelly Holmes hides a battle with self-harming which has plagued her for years.

In a moving and candid interview, the glamorous Olympic champion has admitted she began cutting herself in the year before winning her remarkable double gold at the Athens Olympics in 2004.

She once even considered suicide as a string of gruelling injuries and the pressure of training took its toll. But like the young Team GB athletes who have just lit up the London 2012 games, the star said she never gave up in her search for sporting stardom.

Speaking of her self-harming battle, former British Army judo champion Dame Kelly, 42, said: 'It was desperation. There were lows. Nobody would think someone as strong as me would go through that. I was in a complete and utter mess.

'I don't think it gave me any release. It was just hating myself and my body at that time for letting me down. I was in a training camp in France leading up to the world championships. I was

injured and I think I injured myself nearly every day. I covered the marks up.'

Asked whether she ever considered taking her own life, Dame Kelly replied: 'At one stage, yeah, because I could not cope with the disappointment. The Olympics were the following year and it was my last chance. I mainly cut my arms, chest and top of my leg. It just happened. Before it happened, I never contemplated I could be that kind of person.

'But I am a normal human being and I have emotions and ambition. I don't know why that happened, but there was so much emotion. I still have scars."

This is a shocking but honest account from one of the most recognised sporting personalities in England. Her honesty is part of the reason she is so popular because it connects with real people with real emotions and issues.

Dame Kelly's story is one of the most powerful I have ever come across where the dream was all but over. But because of the power of visualisation she made one last effort to achieve her dream and she made it. She now travels the world inspiring people to never give up and to believe in their dreams.

"If you don't see it before you see it,
you will never see it."

Anon

Studies

Research shows that we change brain structure through repetition of imagining movements. Brain scans of people playing piano versus people imagining playing piano showed the same degree of changes in the same areas of the brain. But to achieve the changes involves repetition of the movements

– real or imaginary. When we stop doing the work, the brain regions shrink again. This is why consistency is vital. You don't become an Olympic champion by going to the gym once. It's important to do consistent visualisation practice to get the best results.

Research was also undertaken in America with the Olympic team, where they studied the impact of visualisation on their athletes. They put electrodes on athletes and measured the muscle movements as they ran a race. They then had the same athletes sit in an armchair and visualise the same race just in their imagination. To their astonishment, they found that the same muscles fired off in the same sequence – with much smaller movements, but they were still there.

This is why Jack Nicklaus, the best golfer in history, never hit a shot in practice or in a match without first seeing every shot in his mind 'like a colour movie'. We now know that he was actually physically practicing the shot even though he was only visualising in his mind. Even though the muscle movements were tiny, they still had an impact in his game. Nowadays all top sports professionals use visualisation techniques to help their game.

In another experiment on visualisation, four schools were chosen across a state in America and the basketball team from each school was split into three groups. They were all assessed for their accuracy in shooting free shots, where they stand 15 feet from the basket and try to get the ball in the basket.

- The first group then had to shoot free shots for an hour a day for 30 days
- The second group had to do nothing
- The third group had to visualise shooting baskets for an hour a day for 30 days.

When they had completed the task, they were assessed

again to see what improvement if any had been achieved. The results were staggering. The first group, who actually practised the shooting, improved by 24%. The second group, who hadn't practised at all, went backwards by 4%. Finally the third group, who only visualised practising, improved by an amazing 23%. This is remarkable but can be attributed to the fact that muscles are firing off even when visualising alone.

More and more business people are using visualisation to help them grow their businesses, with people like Sir Richard Branson, Sir Alan Sugar and Simon Cowell using this technique without even being aware of it. All high achievers dream of what they want to achieve and this is in fact visualisation. They then put the hard work in to make these things happen, but visualisation is the driving force behind their achievements.

"If you can dream it, you can achieve it."

Zig Ziglar

Summary

- Visualisation is a powerful technique to bring things into your life quicker.
- To visualise effectively you have to use your sense of smell, touch, taste and sight.
- You need to feel the feelings you are experiencing to make this more powerful.
- Dame Kelly Holmes used visualisation to create a pathway in her brain which was triggered when she was reminded about her dream as a 14-year-old.
- All top sports people use visualisation to improve their game.
- When we visualise, the muscles fire off in exactly the same

sequence as if we are physically doing the activity, only to a much lesser degree.

- Business people are using visualisation more to help them grow their business.

Action Plan

1. Take something you want to achieve, find an image which represents it and print it off.
2. Look at the picture at least once a day.
3. When you look at the picture, imagine yourself having achieved it.
4. Experience the feelings you have as you visualise and connect with them.
5. What can you hear as you visualise?
6. What can you smell?
7. What can you taste?
8. Can you see movement in the picture?
9. What can you touch?
10. Can you move around and look around you?
11. Repeat this every day and this will come to life in your mind and will increase the chances of you achieving it.

Final Thoughts

Visualisation is a technique used by successful people in all walks of life. If you really want something to come to fruition, then you have to put your imaginative mind to work. See the right result in front of you, rehearse in your mind the game you are going to play, watch yourself accepting your degree at college or walking down that aisle.

There are no limitations – the only limit is your own mind, so start dreaming big.

"Go confidently in the direction of your dreams. Live the life you have imagined."

Henry David Thoreau

Dream Board

A number of experiences or achievements that a person hopes to have or accomplish during their lifetime

Chapter 14

Dream Board – Visualise the future you want

A number of experiences or achievements that a person hopes to have or accomplish during their lifetime

Introduction

There are two key principles I have discovered that have transformed my life. One is the Law of Attraction, and the second is the Vision Board, or as I like to call it, the 'Dream Board'. These two concepts are things that I have bought into in a big way, and they have changed the way I look at life; in particular, the way I look at my future. The Law of Attraction has already been covered in Chapter 12.

The Dream Board is, in principle, a bucket list of all the things you want to achieve before you die – but instead of using words, these dreams are represented in pictures. There is power in pictures and something happens when we put a picture up of something we want to appear in our lives. By looking at the picture regularly, and imagining it as if you already have it, you somehow increase the chances of this appearing in your life.

"Whatever you can do, or dream you can, begin it. Boldness has genius, power and magic in it."

Johann Wolfgang von Goethe

Story

A personal example of effective visualisation, which made me sit up and take notice, was when I put up a picture of a cruise liner as one of the things I wanted to achieve on my

Dream Board. The reason for this image of a cruise liner stems from a situation five years earlier. I was asked to help someone who had decided to leave his company for a year, to give him time to build and design a rowing boat to cross the Atlantic. This was an audacious act by Dave Clarke (not of the Dave Clarke 5) who ran a company with around 70 staff. He had never rowed a boat in his life, although he had sailed across the Atlantic 12 years prior to this.

He wondered, 'how hard could it be,' and was soon to find out. He brought in a CEO to run his company while he was away for the year, and this CEO knew me and my area of expertise. He asked if I could help Dave so I proceeded to work with him on visualisation and the subconscious mind. We spent many hours working together as I built up his confidence, getting him to see himself successfully crossing the Atlantic, and getting stronger and faster in the second half. This all happened to such an effect that he was so fast on the last day he actually beat the plane which was waiting to take off and film him coming in. He didn't go back out to get the footage!

Dave is an adventurer and is mentally strong, so it isn't just the visualisation and positive inner voice techniques alone. However, he agrees that it is likely that these sessions helped him get through the very tough times he experienced. As you can imagine, this is one of the toughest challenges in the world and at the time of his crossing there were less than 100 people who had ever crossed the Atlantic on their own. It took Dave 83 days to cross the 3,000 miles to Barbados with blisters, pain, mental anguish and waves as high at 30ft to contend with. To put this in perspective, there are over 4,000 who have climbed Everest.

Working with Dave inspired me to set up my own business to develop my skills in coaching, speaking and training, to inspire people to achieve more in their lives. I started by coaching one to one, then training groups and finally advanced to public speaking. When Dave flew back to England from Barbados, he spoke to someone who told him that he could get a free holiday if he spoke on a cruise liner about his adventure. We spoke about this for a while but it didn't materialise and he went back to running his successful business.

I worked with Dave coaching him over the next five years and during that time we discussed the speaking on a cruise liner idea, but it never happened. Then I had the thought that maybe I could speak on a cruise. I didn't really know if this would be possible or whether there would be any interest in anything I had to say. So I spent time researching the cruise speaking market and found one agency in the south of England which booked all the speakers for 95% of all cruise liners.

The negative side to this was that it would take a long drive down and back, plus an overnight stay. Then there would be a 45 minute audition in front of a panel of three judges to see if I would be taken on by this agency. This was difficult on several fronts including the time it would take and pressure of performance. So because it wasn't urgent, I kept putting it off and got on with building my business.

"Build your own dreams, or someone else will hire you to build theirs."

Farrah Gray

Dream Board Tested

About two years after finding out about the agency, I

discovered the potential of visualisation and the Dream Board, and decided to develop my own to test this out. To do this I had to go to a peaceful place and spend time in a relaxed state and simply write down a bucket list of all the things I wanted to achieve before I was too old. The list contained things like people I would like to meet, things I wanted to own, people I could help, new skills I wanted to learn and things that would make other people happy.

Once I had the list written down I then spent time pruning it to make sure that each thing on it meant a lot to me. I found pictures that best represented each of these dreams, stuck them on a board and put the board on my bedroom wall. To give this even better impact I then took a photograph of the board and printed out an A4 version which I laminated and put in my work bag.

Every morning I would spend time reading motivation books and then I would spend 20 minutes visualising every one of my 24 dreams as if they had already happened. I would use the techniques I have described in this book – Including the senses of hearing, touch, taste, smell and sight – to bring the visualisations to life. The senses really improve the experience and lock the image in. It's then that things start to happen.

One of the images on my Dream Board was a cruise liner, and every day I would imagine myself speaking on the liner, seeing my audience enjoying themselves. I would see myself in my cabin, eating the wonderful food. As I did this on a daily basis, I was locking the image in and was also locking the image into my subconscious, which would then start to work on this without me being aware consciously.

Then one day about three weeks after I started this process,

I found myself with the phone in my hand dialling the agency on the south coast. The operator answered and put me through to the owner. He was in and answered my call. We spoke for a while and, while it was touch and go whether my subject matter would be suitable for a cruise liner, he suggested I came down to have an audition, which I agreed to.

To this day, I have no idea what inspired me to pick that phone up that day and make the call. What I do know however is that I am delighted that I did. I went down to the south coast later that month and had the audition in front of those judges. Even though there was still a little concern that my subject matter wouldn't be great for the older cruise liner passenger they said they would take me on. They told me that within six months I would be given a cruise to either the Mediterranean or the Canaries. The long journey down and the time taken out of my day to day business was a real pain. Because of this I know for a fact that if I hadn't put it on my Dream Board it would still be a dream.

Within six months, I did indeed get the call to say that they had a cruise liner for me but to my astonishment and delight it was a two-week cruise to the Caribbean! This was an unexpected bonus and what a trip it was! This story doesn't end there, as now that I am on their books I am likely to get a cruise every year. All this happened because I put the picture of a cruise liner on my Dream Board and visualised it every day.

There are several other things which I have ticked off my Dream Board and am now putting new dreams on to see if these come into my life.

It is hard to give concrete evidence as to how this works,

but what I do know is that the people I have spoken to who have a Dream Board seem to achieve a lot of things on their boards as well. They can't necessarily explain how it works, but they seem to agree that something changes when they actually visualise the dreams on a regular basis.

Why Does it Work?

One thing that most people agree on is that the brain is an incredible organ. One of the most difficult to conceive parts of your brain is a small section identified as the Reticular Activating System. This tiny portion of the human brain is the size of your little finger and it can actually have a major role in, and effect on, your life in general.

At any given time, during your daily activities, your mind is bombarded with millions of bits of sensory stimulations from the physical environment. Sounds, smells, tastes, sights and feelings are continually being downloaded into your system, and your mind needs a way to filter that information. This is the purpose of the RAS and the reason it came into being.

The Reticular Activating System sits in your brain and acts as a filter which adapts to different types of situation and reacts instantly. The RAS can be seen as a bouncer at the door of your mind. Your beliefs tell the RAS what is or what is not important, chiefly making a list of all the information invited. Your RAS then acts like the club bouncer, letting whoever is on the list in and thrusting the rest onto the curb.

Of those millions of bits of information cited earlier your RAS only lets around 130 pieces per second in to your conscious mind. That's about all that your central nervous system can handle at one time. The details you let in are the ones that you have decided over the years to be important enough for yourself.

This is where the work comes in, and the amazing results that follow. Over 30 days, if you think about it and imagine yourself experiencing something new, or affirming an additional, recent belief like, 'the world is full of incredible people,' slowly but surely you are moulding your filter so that this new statement is having access to your mind and a new mindset is taking shape.

As you visualise the things on your Dream Board that you want to achieve, you bring these things to the attention of your RAS and the door keeper lets these in. An example of this is Dubai, which is somewhere I am very keen to go to speak, train or coach. I have the Burg Kaleefa and the Burg Al-Arab hotels on my board, as well as a large speaking auditorium, and I visualise myself every morning in Dubai speaking inside these hotels.

The result of this is that I now have five solid contacts in Dubai, and when I go there later this year I will have great potential to make further contacts and potentially secure some work out there. My basketball background should be of interest, combined with my expertise on Mental Resilience. My visualisation has caused me to 'educate' my RAS to alert me whenever Dubai is mentioned and I have observed this at network meetings and speaking with clients and other contacts.

There is science behind the Dream Board concept as well as good old fashioned 'goal setting'. Through my personal experience, to me this is a step beyond goal setting and far more powerful.

Summary

- The Law of Attraction states that you attract what you send out whether good or bad.
- If you focus on something long enough, you will start to

bring it towards you.

- The Dream Board is a way of focusing on the positive things you want in life.
- To bring things into your world visualise them every day with feeling.
- Be very clear about what you want and believe you will receive them.
- The more you feel the emotions, the quicker the things you want will materialise.
- The Reticular Activating System picks out the important things according to your belief system and lets them through, blocking out other information.
- It acts like a bouncer, only letting through the information helpful to you.
- Get your belief system right and the RAS will help you get what you want.
- The RAS can rewire your mind and very rationally take you head first into the life of your dreams.

Action Plan

1. Go away for a day or two and write a bucket list of all the things you want in your life.
2. Find pictures to represent each of the dreams you have and copy and paste them onto an A4 sheet.
3. Print the sheet off and look at it every day, visualising as though you already have it.
4. Make sure that you visualise each of the pictures using your senses of smell, hearing, touch, taste and sight and really feel the feelings you have inside.
5. Visualise at least one dream in detail every day using all your senses.
6. Believe that you can receive these things and that you deserve them.
7. Be grateful for everything you have in your life right now to stay in a positive state.

Final Thoughts

A Dream Board is a visual representation of the dreams and goals we want to achieve in our life. It's less about specific things we want than it is about who we want to be in this world. It is a simple and enjoyable way of focusing our minds on the things which are most important to us and which we want to come into our lives.

As we all know – 'a picture is worth a thousand words'.

"If you can dream it, you can do it."

Walt Disney

Gratitude

The quality of being thankful; readiness to show appreciation for and to return kindness

Chapter 15

Gratitude

The quality of being thankful; readiness to show appreciation for and to return kindness

Introduction

Everyone has times when they feel thankful for a person or a situation. These moments of thinking about the past in a positive way give us a good feeling. Gratitude, or appreciation for the good things that happen in life, is a really important part of building happiness.

You can be thankful for anything in your life that makes you feel positive on some level. Some bigger things could include friends and family, achieving a goal, appreciating where you live, or the opportunities you have in life.

However, you don't need to limit your gratitude to big picture ideas. Positive things that seem small and happen every day are also worth focusing on, such as a great day out, a funny joke you heard from a friend, a family pet, or a sunny day.

Gratitude matters. A grateful heart is a contented heart. Gratitude opens the door to simplicity and happiness. A person who is grateful for the things they own will care for them, enjoy them, and waste less energy seeking more. They will experience contentment in the gifts they already possess rather than looking outside themselves for more.
One thing I am really grateful for is an opportunity that was given to me by Nicola Burley, the Director of Enterprise and Operations at the Galleries of Justice. She gave me an opportunity to speak to her staff about three years ago when I was still relatively unknown. On the back of that, I was booked to speak at their Unique Connections Networking

event which resulted in some good work for me.

I think back to the days when I was building my business. I am grateful for those people who took a risk booking me, not really knowing what I was going to deliver – this gave me the opportunity to improve. I have lost count of the number of talks I have given to Rotary Clubs which gave me the chance to practise my speaking skills.

When I think about it, I am so grateful to so many people for all they have done for me, and I never run out of things to be grateful for. I have a Gratitude Journal, in which I write down the things I am grateful for, and every morning I read through some of them and feel the feelings of gratitude. This not only feels good, but it gets me in the right frame of mind for the day.

Gratitude is more than just feeling good. It helps people become less aggressive by enhancing their empathy. Gratitude puts situations into perspective. When we can see the good as well as the bad, it becomes more difficult to complain and stay stuck.

More than anything, gratitude is the emotion of friendship. It is part of a psychological system that causes people to raise their estimates of how much value they hold in the eyes of another person. Gratitude is what happens when someone does something that causes you to realise that you matter more to that person than you thought you did.

***"This is a wonderful day.
I've never seen this one before."***

Maya Angelou

Have you ever been in a frustrating situation that has ruined everyone's mood for the evening? There is a simple way of showing gratitude in any circumstances, which can turn things around dramatically.

Story

I remember a time when I ordered a Chinese takeaway for dinner. My family had plans for that night, which meant we would only be together for an hour before everyone had to run off to do other things. We picked up the food and drove home, but when we opened the bag, we realised that the restaurant had forgotten to include one of the main dishes from our order.

In the grand scheme of things, this isn't a huge deal. That said, at that moment we had an issue – either someone had to drive back and get the food, or we had to settle for eating half of the dinner we ordered. It seems frivolous in retrospect, but this is exactly the type of little upset that can ruin the mood and pull everyone into a negative spiral – especially when you are in a rush.

I volunteered to drive back to the restaurant and pick up the missing food. When I returned 35 minutes later, we finally sat down to eat dinner with about 25 minutes to spare – so basically, it was a rushed evening. The mood in the room was frustrated and stressed. But I had a very simple gratitude habit that came to the rescue.

When I sit down to eat dinner, I say one thing that happened today for which I am grateful. On this particular day, after the frantic rush of the evening, I said that I was grateful for my family being together at breakfast that day. This was because it allowed us to spend time together that we didn't get to spend later in the evening.

As everyone else contributed their own grateful moment

> *from the day the energy completely reset in the room. It was like we all breathed a deep sigh and said, 'okay, that was annoying, but we're over it now. We live a good life and it's time to move on and enjoy the moment.'*

"A truly rich man is one whose children run into his arms when his hands are empty."

Unknown

Why is this Gratitude Habit so Effective?

- It is a really good idea at least once a day to force yourself into a positive frame of mind. When we sit down for dinner, we are forced to think about the good in our lives for at least a few seconds.
- The individual impact of any one piece of gratitude is small, but the cumulative effect is huge. You begin to realize that nearly every day is a good day (at least in a small way).
- You start to realize how insignificant monetary things are for your day-to-day happiness.
- This habit is ridiculously small, so it is easy to stick with.
- I anchored my gratitude habit onto my habit of eating dinner each night. It is so much easier to build a new habit into your lifestyle when you choose the right trigger.

Why Practise Gratitude?

- **Because it reminds you of the positive things in your life.**
  It makes you happy about the people in your life whether they're loved ones, or just a stranger you met who was kind to you in some way.
- **Because it turns bad things into good things.**
  Having problems at work? Be grateful you have work. Be grateful you have challenges, and that life isn't boring. Be grateful that you can learn from these challenges and

that they make you stronger.

- **Because it reminds you of what's important.**
  It's hard to complain about the little things when you give thanks that your children are alive and healthy. It's hard to get stressed out over paying bills when you are grateful there is a roof over your head.
- **Because it reminds you to thank others.**
  The simple act of saying 'thank you' to someone can make a big difference in that person's life. Whether that's calling them, emailing them or visiting to say thank you, people like being appreciated for who they are and what they do. It costs little, but makes someone else happy, and making someone else happy will make you happy.

Psychologist Robert Emmons, perhaps the world's leading scientific expert on gratitude, argues that gratitude has three stages:

1. **Recognising** what we are grateful for
2. **Acknowledging** it
3. **Appreciating** it.

Emmons and other researchers see a social dimension as being especially important to gratitude. It requires us to see how we've been supported and affirmed by other people and encourages us not only to appreciate gifts, but to repay them.

"Gratitude is a vaccine, an antitoxin, and an antiseptic."

John Henry Jowet

Studies

According to research published by the American Psychological Association, lead author Paul J. Mills, PhD stated that recognising and giving thanks for the good things in life can result in better health. Paul J. Mills is Professor of family medicine and public health at the University of California. Some of the reported health effects included:

1. Less depression;
2. Higher quality sleep;
3. Less fatigue;
4. More self-efficacy (belief in one's ability to handle a situation);
5. Less inflammation.

The study included 186 men and women who had received a diagnosis of Stage B heart failure at least three months before the study. According to Mills, this stage has significant therapeutic value because it's the chance to halt the progression of the disease before it worsens to Stage C, in which risk of death is five times higher.

Using standard psychological tests, the participants were scored on gratitude and spiritual well-being. The team then analysed those scores and compared them to the patients' results for depressive symptom severity, sleep quality, fatigue, self-efficacy and inflammatory markers.

They found that the higher the gratitude scores: the better the mood, the higher quality of sleep, more self-efficacy and less inflammation, which can exacerbate heart failure.

Exploring further, the researchers asked some of the group to use a journal and to jot down daily three things for which they were thankful for, for eight weeks. While all of the patients continued to receive regular clinical care during the time, the ones who recorded what they were thankful for improved even more.

'We found that those patients who kept gratitude journals for those eight weeks showed reductions in circulating levels of several important inflammatory biomarkers, as well as an increase in heart rate variability while they wrote. Improved heart rate variability is considered a measure of reduced cardiac risk,' said Mills.

'It seems that a more grateful heart is indeed a more healthy heart,' he added.

Recent studies have concluded that the expression of gratitude can have profound and positive effects on our health, our moods and even the survival of our marriages. A growing body of research shows that gratitude is truly amazing in its physical and psychosocial benefits.

A study on gratitude was conducted by Robert A. Emmons, PhD, at the University of California and his colleague Mike McCullough, at the University of Miami. Here they randomly assigned participants to one of three tasks. Each week, participants kept a short journal:

1. One group briefly described five things they were grateful for that had occurred in the past week;
2. The second group recorded five daily hassles from the previous week that displeased them;
3. The third neutral group was asked to list five events or circumstances that affected them, but they were not told whether to focus on the positive or on the negative.

10 weeks later, participants in the first group felt better about their lives as a whole and were a full 25% happier than the second group. They reported fewer health complaints and exercised an average of one and a half hours more.

In a later study by Emmons, people were asked to write every day about things for which they were grateful. Not surprisingly, this daily practice led to greater increases in gratitude than the weekly journaling did in the first study.

But the results showed another benefit: Participants in the

gratitude group also reported offering others more emotional support and help with a personal problem, indicating that the gratitude exercise increased their goodwill towards others.

There's an old saying that **'if you've forgotten the language of gratitude, you'll never be on speaking terms with happiness'.** It turns out this isn't just a fluffy idea. Several studies have shown depression to be inversely correlated to gratitude. It seems that the more grateful a person is, the less depressed they are.

Philip Watkins, a clinical psychologist at Eastern Washington University, found that clinically depressed individuals showed significantly lower gratitude (nearly 50% less) than non-depressed controls.

Dr. John Gottman at the University of Washington has been researching marriages for two decades. With 90% accuracy, Gottman says he can predict, often after only three minutes of observation, which marriages are likely to flourish and which are likely to flounder.

The formula is that for every negative expression (a complaint, frown, put-down, and expression of anger) there needs to be about five positive ones (smiles, compliments, laughter, expressions of appreciation and gratitude). The conclusion of all that research, he states, is that unless a couple is able to maintain a high ratio of positive to negative encounters (five to one, or greater), it is likely the marriage will end.

Summary

- There is evidence that practicing gratitude provides many benefits.
- People who regularly practise gratitude experience more positive emotions and feel more alive.
- Grateful people experience more contentment.

- They often sleep better.
- They express more compassion and kindness.
- They have enhanced empathy and reduced aggression.
- They can put situations into perspective more easily.
- They tend to have stronger immune systems.
- They experience the 'emotion of friendship'.

Gratitude doesn't need to be reserved only for momentous occasions. You might express gratitude after receiving a promotion at work, but you can also be thankful for something as simple as a delicious piece of cake.

Action Plan

Feeling grateful just happens sometimes, but you can also make a special effort to increase how often you feel it:

1. **Intentionally choose gratitude**
   Change your perspective. Notice your daily world from a point of gratitude and you will be amazed at all the goodness we take for granted.

2. **Switch a negative trait to a positive one**
   If you identify with a negative trait, change it. For example, the cold office at work becomes the office with the great view.

3. **Give at least one compliment daily**
   It can be to a person or it can be asking someone to share your appreciation of something.

4. **Sound genuinely happy to hear from the people who phone you**
   Whether the caller responds with surprise or delight, they'll know you value speaking with them.

5. **When you find yourself in a bad situation, ask: 'What can I learn?'**
   When you look back on this without emotion, what will you be grateful for?

6. **Gratitude requires humility**
   Become involved in a cause that is important to you; donate money, time or talent.

Final Thoughts

Feeling grateful is a skill we can develop with practice. To build positive momentum towards a more happy and fulfilling life, try these simple things:

1. **Keep a daily journal** of three things you are thankful for. This works well first thing in the morning, or just before you go to bed.
2. **Make it a practice** to tell a spouse, partner or friend something you appreciate about them every day.
3. **Look in the mirror** when you are brushing your teeth, and think about something you have done well recently or something you like about yourself.

"Be thankful for what you have; you'll end up having more. If you concentrate on what you don't have, you will never, ever have enough."

Oprah Winfrey

"'Be thankful that you don't already have everything you desire.
If you did, what would there be to look forward to?

Be thankful when you don't know something,
For it gives you the opportunity to learn.

Be thankful for the difficult times.
During those times you grow.

Be thankful for your limitations,
Because they give you opportunities for improvement.

Be thankful for each new challenge,
Because it will build your strength and character.

Be thankful for your mistakes.
They will teach you valuable lessons.

Be thankful when you're tired and weary,
Because it means you've made a difference.

It is easy to be thankful for the good things.
A life of rich fulfilment comes to those who are also thankful for the setbacks.

Gratitude can turn a negative into a positive.
Find a way to be thankful for your troubles and they can become your blessings."

Anon

Mindfulness

A mental state achieved by focusing one's awareness on the present moment, while calmly acknowledging and accepting one's feelings, thoughts, and bodily sensations

Chapter 16

Mindfulness

A mental state achieved by focusing one's awareness on the present moment, while calmly acknowledging and accepting one's feelings, thoughts, and bodily sensations

Introduction

Have you ever been driving somewhere and arrived at your destination, only to realise you remember nothing about your journey? Or started eating a chocolate bar, taken a couple of bites, then noticed all you had left was an empty wrapper in your hand? Or maybe it is a gorgeous day, but you don't even see what is right in front of you?

These are common examples of 'mindlessness', or 'going on autopilot', when we go through our days without really paying attention to much of anything. Nobody else would suspect that we are hardly there; almost nobody notices, probably because they're on autopilot, too.

Sometimes it doesn't seem to matter much. At other times it really does matter, because life begins to feel shallower if you spend too much time being unaware. As humans, we are often 'not present' in our own lives.
Human minds are easily distracted, habitually examining past events and trying to anticipate the future, and constantly multi-tasking. It is easy to lose awareness of the present moment as we become lost in our efforts to juggle work, home, finances, and other conflicting demands.

Becoming more aware of our thoughts, emotions and sensations may not sound like an obviously helpful thing to do. However, learning to do this in a way that suspends judgement and self-criticism can have an incredibly positive impact on our lives.

Mindfulness is a way of paying attention to whatever is happening in our lives by being 'fully in the moment'. It will not eliminate life's pressures, but it can help us respond to them in a calmer manner that benefits our heart, head and body. It helps us recognise and change habitual emotional and physiological reactions to everyday events. It provides us with a scientifically researched approach to cultivating clarity, insight, and understanding.

"Life isn't about getting and having, it's about giving and being."

Kevin Kruse

Practicing mindfulness allows us to be fully present in our life and work, and improve our quality of life.
Mark Williams, Professor of clinical psychology at the Oxford Mindfulness Centre, says that mindfulness means knowing directly what is going on inside and outside ourselves, moment by moment. Mindfulness can be an antidote to the 'tunnel vision' that can develop in our daily lives, especially when we are busy, stressed or tired.

He says that an important part of mindfulness is reconnecting with our bodies and the sensations they experience. This means waking up to the sights, sounds, smells and tastes of the present moment. That might be something as simple as the feel of a banister as we walk upstairs.

Another important part of mindfulness is an awareness of our thoughts and feelings as they happen, moment to moment. Awareness of this kind doesn't start by trying to change or fix anything. It's about allowing ourselves to see the present moment clearly. When we do that, it can positively change the way we see ourselves and our lives.

"Your vision will become clear only when you look into your heart. Who looks outside, dreams. Who looks inside, awakens."

Carl Jung

What is Mindfulness?

Mindfulness has its origins in ancient Buddhist meditation practices. However, a secular practice of mindfulness has entered the Western mainstream in recent years.

The acknowledged founder of modern day mindfulness is Jon Kabat-Zinn, who started the Stress Reduction Clinic at the University of Massachusetts Medical School in the late 1970s. Since then over 18,000 people have completed the MBSR (Mindfulness Based Stress Reduction) Programme to help with conditions as diverse as:

- Chronic pain
- Heart disease
- Anxiety
- Psoriasis
- Sleep problems
- Depression.

Studies have documented the physical and mental health benefits of mindfulness in general and MBSR in particular. This has inspired countless programmes in the US to adapt the MBSR model for schools, prisons, hospitals, veterans centres and beyond.

Story

James was 17, in the sixth form and on his way to class after a lunch break. He walked just 100 meters out of the lunch room when suddenly he was overcome by an intense fear. He started shaking and feeling nauseous and it took him15 minutes before he felt like he could actually move. These attacks happened on a few further occasions and each time he was sent home, only to be met by his father telling him that he thought James was faking it. To make matters worse, his mother, sister and other family members simply didn't talk about it, which made him feel very isolated.

In his second year of university, things got worse. His anxiety was getting so bad that he couldn't attend classes, and conversely missing lessons fuelled his anxiety because he knew that the material he was missing would be on the exam. He suspended his studies and returned home, and became agoraphobic; spending most days indoors reading, watching TV or playing video games. Oddly he became happy with his little rut but at his worst he wasn't able to make a 10-minute car journey to visit his gran. The severity of his anxiety had worsened, coupled with fear and unpleasant physical symptoms.

During this period, he went through different types of treatment such as a support group, a one-to-one version of the support group and Cognitive Behaviour Therapy – none of which helped with his symptoms. Mindfulness was first suggested to him and he was initially sceptical. He thought it seemed very 'touchy feely' – like a theoretical, homoeopathic angle on treatment. He wondered how on earth slowing his breathing and thinking 'happy thoughts' could help him in the long term?

However, his opinion of mindfulness completely changed after the first session. Since practising mindfulness, he has found that he is more positive generally. It has given him a new perspective on what's important in his life and he feels like he is a stronger, more resilient person in the face of life's daily stresses and pressures. He has gone from trying to block everything out, to dealing with it as and when it occurs, and through the most effective means available to him at the time.

Today, he builds mindfulness into his everyday life. He finds breathing, imagery and meditation exercises most useful and tends to do these once or twice a day. The biggest shock for him was that he could practise anywhere, anytime, and often without other people knowing. It's actually very empowering to know that you can control your reactions and feelings in any situation without others even being aware of it.

Jon Kabat-Zinn's definition of mindfulness is quite specific:

"Mindfulness means paying attention in a particular way; on purpose, in the present moment, and non-judgmentally."

1. Paying attention 'on purpose'

Mindfulness involves a specific and conscious direction of our awareness. We sometimes talk about 'mindfulness' and 'awareness' as if they were interchangeable terms. However, to be mindful we have to be purposefully aware of ourselves, not just vaguely and habitually aware. Knowing that you are eating a meal is not the same as eating a meal mindfully.

Let's look at that example of eating a bit more. When we

are purposefully aware of eating, we are consciously being aware of the process of eating. We're deliberately noticing the sensations and our responses to those sensations. We're noticing the mind wandering, and when it does wander we purposefully bring our attention back.

When we're eating unmindfully we may, in theory, be aware of what we're doing. However, we are probably thinking about a hundred other things at the same time, or we may also be watching TV. So a very small part of our awareness is absorbed with eating, and we may be only barely aware of the physical sensations and even less aware of our thoughts and emotions.

This purposefulness is a very important part of mindfulness. Having the purpose of staying with our experience, whether that's the breath, or a particular emotion, or something as simple as eating, means that we are actively shaping the mind.

2. Paying attention 'in the present moment'

Left to itself the mind wanders through all kinds of thoughts – including thoughts of anger, craving, depression, revenge, self-pity, and so on. As we indulge in these kinds of thoughts, we reinforce those emotions in our hearts and cause ourselves to suffer. Mostly these thoughts are about the past or future. The past no longer exists; the future is just a fantasy until it happens.

In mindfulness, we're concerned with noticing what's going on right now. By intentionally directing our awareness away from thoughts about the past or future and towards the 'anchor' of our present moment experience, we decrease their effect on our lives. We create instead a space of freedom where calmness and contentment can grow.

That doesn't mean we can no longer think about the past or future, but when we do so we do so mindfully. We need to be aware that right now we're thinking about the past or future.

3. Paying attention 'non-judgmentally'

Mindfulness is an emotionally non-reactive state. We don't judge that one experience is good and that one is bad. Or if we do make those judgements we simply notice them and let go of them. We don't get upset about what we are experiencing; we simply accept whatever arises. We observe it mindfully – we notice it arising, passing through us, and ceasing to exist.

Whether it's a pleasant experience or a painful experience we treat it the same way. We are aware that certain experiences are pleasant and some are unpleasant, but on an emotional level we simply don't react.

"The moment one gives close attention to anything, even a blade of grass, it becomes a mysterious, awesome, indescribably magnificent world in itself."

Henry Miller

Benefits of Mindfulness

There have been many studies related to mindfulness, which suggest mindfulness training may:

- **Improve memory and academic performance.** In one study, students who did attention-building exercises had increased focus, less mind-wandering, better short-term memory and better performance on exams.

- **Help with losing weight and eating healthier foods.** Mindful eating means paying attention to each bite and eating slowly, at the same time being aware of all your senses. Participants in mindfulness studies ate fewer calories when they were hungrier than the control groups.

- **Lead to better decision-making.**
  Some experiments associated mindfulness meditation with being less prone to our tendency to stick with lost causes, because of the time and effort already invested, such as with a bad relationship or a poor job. Studies suggest that mindfulness helps us focus on what is most important.

- **Lower stress and help cope with chronic health issues.**
  Studies showed that mindfulness increased both mental and physical well-being in patients with chronic pain, cancer, and heart disease.

- **Improve immunity and create positive brain changes.**
  Researchers measured brain activity before and after volunteers were trained in the technique of mindfulness meditation for eight weeks. It was found that it increases the density of grey matter in brain regions linked to learning, memory, emotion regulation and empathy. Studies suggested that mindfulness changes our brains.

"Life is not measured by the number of breaths we take, but by the moments that take our breath away."

Maya Angelou

Summary

- As humans, we often exist on 'autopilot' on a daily basis.
- Mindfulness allows us to be fully present in our life and work.
- Practising mindfulness can improve our quality of life.
- An important part of mindfulness is reconnecting with

our bodies and the sensations they experience.
- It helps us to recognise and change habitual emotional and physiological reactions to everyday events.
- It can help us respond to pressures in a calmer manner that benefits our heart, head and body.
- It provides us with a scientifically researched approach to cultivating clarity, insight and understanding.
- It can help with specific issues such as academic performance, memory, decision-making and potentially weight loss.

Action Plan

1. **Remind yourself to take notice of your thoughts, feelings, bodily sensations and the world around you as you go about your daily life.** Notice the sensations, the food you eat and the air moving past your ears as you walk. This has huge power to interrupt the 'autopilot' and to give you new perspectives on life.
2. **Pick a time during which you decide to be aware of the sensations created by the world around you.** For example, this could be the morning journey to work or a walk at lunchtime. Try new things, such as sitting in a different seat in meetings or going somewhere new for lunch, to help you notice the world in a new way.
3. **Notice the thoughts buzzing round in your head.** Just observe them without trying to change them, like watching leaves floating past in a stream. This takes practice.
4. **Pay close attention to your breathing,** especially when you're feeling intense emotions.
5. **Really notice what you're sensing in a given moment.** Notice the sights, sounds, and smells that ordinarily slip by without reaching your conscious awareness.
6. **Your thoughts and emotions are fleeting and do**

not define you. Recognising this important insight can free you from negative thought patterns.

7. **Tune in to your body's physical sensations,** from the water hitting your skin in the shower to the way your body rests in your office chair.
8. **To develop mindfulness skills** in everyday life, you can try these practical exercises:

a. The body scan.
Focus your attention along your body, from the toes to the top of your head, trying to be aware and accepting of whatever you sense in these body parts, without controlling or changing those feelings.

b. The raisin exercise.
Slowly use all of your senses, one after another, to observe a raisin in great detail – from the way it feels in your hand, to the way its taste bursts on your tongue. This helps you focus on the present moment.

c. Walking meditation.
Focus on the movement of your body as you take step after step, your feet touching and leaving the ground. This exercise is often practised walking back and forth along a path 10 paces long, though it can be practised along any path.

d. Loving-kindness meditation.
This involves extending feelings of compassion toward people, starting with yourself then branching out to someone close to you. Then to an acquaintance, then to someone giving you a hard time, and finally to all people everywhere.

Final Thoughts

In short, mindfulness is about tuning in and being more aware of every experience – to be fully living in the moment. This part of William Blake's poem perfectly describes this kind of attentiveness:

"To see a world in a grain of sand
And a heaven in a wild flower
Hold infinity in the palm of your hand
And eternity in an hour."

William Blake, Auguries of Innocence

Energy Levels

Energy is your capacity to do work. It provides the fuel that enables you to weather the storm effectively and to bounce back resiliently

Chapter 17

Energy Levels – How to stay energised

Energy is your capacity to do work. It provides the fuel that enables you to weather the storm effectively and to bounce back resiliently

Introduction

As I write this chapter, there has just been some research released that confirms what I have been saying for some time, which is that sugar and carbohydrates are the real enemies of good health. Apparently, the NHS didn't get it quite right and thought that the real problem was fat. However, the latest research indicates that natural fats like butter and cream are not bad for us, but that carbohydrates – especially sugar – are the real problem.

So, the food industry was asked to reduce fat in all its products. But to improve the taste of these low-fat products they increased the sugar content, and that is when the obesity and diabetes problems started to increase. And they have continued to increase to the horrific levels we see today.

I attended a talk by a nutrition expert who showed us all the evidence as to what happens to the carbohydrates we consume. He informed us that the latest science has shown that sugar and carbohydrates turn into glucose in the blood, which we need to function. This glucose is then distributed to all the organs that require it, but here is the important bit: the excess glucose turns to fat. He said that basically this is the main way we put on unwanted fat, particularly around the waist, which is the danger area.

He recommended that we avoid a big breakfast and graze on unsalted nuts like walnuts, hazelnuts, brazils, cashews and almonds, plus some fruit, and avoid carbs wherever possible. He also recommended that we eat a reasonably sized evening meal as this helps us go to sleep.

So, the best way to get rid of belly fat is to stop eating sugar and carbohydrates (or drastically reduce the intake of these). By stopping the excess glucose turning to fat, the body then uses up the fat stored around the belly and, therefore, this fat starts to disappear. You will find that on a low sugar/carbohydrate diet your weight will drop and you will feel neither over-full nor hungry.

I have discovered in two short weeks that I have lost a few pounds, have much more energy during the day and, most importantly, don't get that energy dip I used to get in the afternoons. I feel really good in myself and don't feel full all the time like I used to. I am in a more positive state about myself and, by the Law of Attraction that brings in more good feelings – and on it continues.

"Our bodies are our gardens – our wills are our gardeners."

William Shakespeare

Sugar Cravings

Of all the carbohydrates we consume, sugar is the worst culprit of all and it is very addictive. Does that morning Danish pastry leave you craving another treat two hours later? Do you grab a chocolate bar to cope with your afternoon slump – and then reach for a coke to get out of your post-slump slump?

If you've found that munching sugary snacks just makes you crave more sugary snacks, you're not alone. Eating lots of simple carbohydrates – without the backup of proteins or fats

– can quickly satisfy hunger and give your body a short-term energy boost, but almost as quickly they leave you hungry again and craving more.

Why do we Crave Sugar?

- The appetite for sweet things may be hardwired. Christine Gerbstadt, MD, RD, a dietitian and American Dietetic Association spokeswoman states that, 'sweet is the first taste humans prefer from birth.' Carbohydrates stimulate the release of the feel-good brain chemical serotonin. Sugar is a carbohydrate, but carbohydrates come in other forms, too, such as whole grains, fruits, and vegetables.
- The taste of sugar also releases endorphins. These calm and relax us, and offer a natural 'high', says Susan Moores, MS, RD, a registered dietician and nutrition consultant in St. Paul, Minnesota.
- Sweets simply taste good. Rewarding ourselves with sweet treats, which can make us crave them even more, reinforces that preference.

It is fine to indulge in a sweet treat now and then, but the problems arise when we over-consume sugary foods. This is something that is very easy to do, as sugar is added to many processed foods including bread, yogurt, juices and sauces.

The American Heart Association recommends limiting added sugars to about six teaspoons per day for women and nine for men, but Americans over-consume significantly, averaging about 22 teaspoons of added sugars per day.

Most of us have felt that urge, the unstoppable craving driving us to seek out something sweet and devour it in a flash. That uncontrollable desire for cookies, cake or ice cream or that whole basket of bread calling to us to finish it off.

Why do we overeat? Why does that biscuit have such power

over you, even though you know it will make you fat and sick? Is it an indication of your lack of willpower, moral weakness, or is it a powerful hardwired brain response over which you have little control?

Debate has raged recently about whether junk food, that over-processed, hyper-palatable food, is addictive. A new study published in the American Journal of Clinical Nutrition suggests that, in fact, higher sugar, higher glycemic foods can be addictive.

Study

David Ludwig, author of Ending the Food Fight, and his colleagues at Harvard, did a very sophisticated study. They showed that foods with more sugar, foods that raise blood sugar even more than table sugar, such as white flour, white potatoes and refined starch, have what is called a high glycemic index. This triggers a special region in the brain called the nucleus accumbens that is known to be 'ground zero' for conventional addiction, such as gambling or drug abuse.

Part of the reason almost 70% of Americans are overweight or one in two Americans have pre-diabetes or Type 2 diabetes may not be gluttony, lack of willpower or absence of personal responsibility. It may simply be biological addiction.

Many previous studies have shown how this region of the brain, the pleasure centre, lights up in response to images of eating sugary, processed or junk food. This is interesting data, but it's not hard proof of addiction as many of these studies used very different foods as a comparison. If you compare cheesecake to boiled vegetables, there are varying reasons the pleasure centre can light up – it looks better, tastes better or is a nicer colour.

This new study took on the difficult task of proving the biology of sugar addiction. The researchers did a randomized, blinded crossover study using the most rigorous research design to ward off any criticism.

They took 12 overweight or obese men between the ages of 18 and 35, and gave each a low sugar or low glycemic index milkshake (37%). Then, four hours later they measured the activity of the brain region (nucleus accumbens) that controls addiction. They also measured blood sugar and hunger levels.

Then, days later, they had them back for another milkshake. But this time they switched the milkshakes. They were designed to taste exactly the same and be exactly the same in every way except in how much and how quickly it spiked blood sugar. The second milkshake was designed to be high in sugar with a high glycemic index (84%). The shakes had exactly the same amount of calories, protein, fat and carbohydrate. The participants didn't know which milkshake they were getting and their mouth couldn't tell the difference, but their brains could.

Each participant received a brain scan and blood tests for glucose and insulin after each version of the milkshake. They were their own control group.

Without exception, they all had the same response. The high sugar or glycemic index milkshake caused a spike in blood sugar and insulin and an increase in reported hunger and cravings four hours after the shake. Remember – the milkshakes had exactly the same calories, sweetness, texture and macronutrient content. This finding was not surprising and has been shown many times before.

But the breakthrough finding was this: When the high-glycemic shake was consumed, the nucleus accumbens lit up like a Christmas tree. This pattern occurred in every single

participant and was statistically significant.
This study showed two things. Firstly, the body responds quite differently to different calories, even if the protein, fat, carbohydrates and taste are exactly the same. Secondly, foods that spike blood sugar are biologically addictive.

This game-changing study must force a shift in the conversation about obesity. In America, there are 600,000 processed foods in the marketplace, 80% of which have added hidden sugar. In fact, some animal studies show that sugar is eight times as addictive as cocaine, which explains the growing problem worldwide.

"The healthy man is the thin man. But you don't need to go hungry for it: Remove the flours, starches and sugars; that's all."

Samael Aun Weor

Summary

- Sugar and carbohydrates are the real health problem.
- Sugar and carbohydrates turn into glucose in the blood, and the excess turns into fat.
- To improve the taste of low-fat products the sugar content has been increased.
- Our appetite for sugar and sweet things may be hardwired.
- Sugar releases endorphins that calm and relax us, and offer a natural 'high'.
- Foods that spike blood sugar are biologically addictive.
- Sugar can be much more addictive than cocaine.
- Sugar gives us a high, but it is followed by an energy low within four hours or less.
- High sugar content in the blood makes the pancreas work harder to produce insulin.
- Eventually, the pancreas stops producing insulin, and Type 2 diabetes is the result.

- Sugar and carbohydrates are the single biggest reason for the increase in obesity.
- The most effective way to reduce belly fat is to reduce sugar and carbohydrates.
- To maintain constant energy all day, avoid sugars and starches and replace them with unsalted nuts, some fruit and low sugar health bars.
- Eat a banana mid-afternoon, rather than a chocolate bar or biscuit, to boost energy

Experts say that it takes 28 days to detox from most addictive substances, and refined carbohydrates, such as white flour and white rice, are no exception.

White carbohydrates are so addictive because of the chemicals that travel from the stomach to the part of the brain where you produce dopamine, a hormone and neurotransmitter that affects the brain's pleasure and reward centres. Once these areas of the brain are stimulated, you'll keep on wanting more of the addictive substance, whether it's alcohol, drugs or carbohydrates.

Too many refined carbohydrates, such as pastries, French fries or processed snack foods like crisps and pretzels, are simply toxic for your body. They're often responsible for the dangerous fat you can carry around your middle that actually inhibits your body's ability to make insulin, which makes you more prone to diabetes. White carbohydrates also increase your risk of cardiovascular disease and even cancer.

Action Plan

This simple 28-day plan can help you break free of carbohydrate addiction. You'll be amazed at how you'll look and feel afterward – you'll have more energy and lose unwanted pounds, especially around your midsection. I've been working on this for less than two weeks and I am amazed how well I feel, how much energy I have and how much belly fat I have lost already. By the way, all sugar products are carbohydrates including chocolate, ice cream, cakes, sweets, and so on.

Week 1: Detox with Fats

Start kicking the habit by throwing out all the carbohydrates in your kitchen. To withstand the symptoms of withdrawal, fill up on healthy fats and don't worry about your calorie intake. The point of this first week is to get off simple carbohydrates. Fats are satiating, which will help diminish hunger pangs and keep you from overeating.

In addition, for this week, none of your food servings should have more than 4 grams of sugar.

Choose healthy fats like olive oil, nuts, avocado, fatty fish such as salmon and flax seeds.

Week 2: Turn White into Brown

Whole grains keep you full longer, stabilise blood sugar, and are loaded with fibre, vitamins, minerals and antioxidants. Plus, a diet rich in whole grains has been tied to lower rates of chronic disease such as diabetes, high blood pressure, high cholesterol and obesity. Restock your pantry with fibre-rich brown carbs such as quinoa, oatmeal, whole wheat bread, brown rice and whole grain pasta

Week 3: Hand to Mouth
At this point, you've been filling up on healthy fats and whole grains. Now you need to focus on portion control. Forget about scales and measuring cups. You can use your hands to measure the right portion size:

Carbohydrates = Fist – A serving of carbs should be about the size of your fist.

Protein = Palm – A serving of meat, poultry or fish should be about the size of your palm.

Fats = Thumb – A serving of fats should be about the size of your thumb.

Fruits and Veggies = Handfuls – For fruits and veggies, grab all you can hold!

Always combine your carbohydrates with fats (but no more than a thumb's worth). This will help you slow sugar absorption and control your weight.

Week 4: Time to Cheat

Pick one day a week to enjoy your favourite white-flour food such as bread, pizza or pasta. Ensure you eat your favourite carbohydrate with fibre such as vegetables, which will also help you better metabolise sugar and keep your weight down. For instance, top your pizza or pasta with a bunch of veggies.

Final Thoughts

Sugar is the core ingredient used by the food industry to make bad ingredients, such as white flour and processed food, taste good. No one wants to be fat or become a drug addict. No one wants their life destroyed by disability or illness. We have policies and laws that protect people from alcohol, tobacco and illegal drugs. Yet sugar and flour (and too much starchy white potatoes and white rice) appear to be no different.

If you consume certain foods even if you are not hungry because of cravings, or worry about cutting down on certain foods. If you feel sluggish from overeating, or have health or social problems because of food issues.Then you should consider your eating habits and whether you may be addicted to sugar, flour and processed food.

There are techniques that can help you to break free of your addiction, and following the 28-day action plan is a simple way to begin to detox. You will quickly start to feel better, look much better and have more energy for life.

Life with very little sugar and carbohydrates is an energised, healthy one. You feel great, you look great and you perform better. It is definitely worth the effort needed to put this into action. I for one can highly recommend it!

"Take care of your body.
It's the only place you have to live."

Jim Rohn

Sleep

The natural periodic suspension of consciousness during which the powers of the body are restored

Chapter 18

Sleep - where dreams come true

The natural periodic suspension of consciousness during which the powers of the body are restored

Introduction

Sleep is far more important than many people realise, and lack of sleep can have very serious consequences. According to the Division of Sleep Medicine at the Harvard Medical School, the short-term productivity gains from missing sleep in order to work are heavily outweighed by the negative effects of sleep deprivation. This effects your mood, ability to focus and access to higher-level brain functions.

New research from the University of Rochester found that when you sleep your brain removes toxic proteins from its neurons. These toxins are by-products of neural activity when you're awake, but your brain can only remove them adequately when you're asleep. So when you don't get enough sleep, the toxic proteins remain in your brain cells, reducing your ability to think.

Effects of Sleep Deprivation

Missing sleep impairs your brain function. Your body overproduces the stress hormone cortisol when it is sleep deprived, which has many negative health effects that come from the damage it does to your immune system.

Some of the effects of sleep deprivation are:

- Memory lapse or loss
- Decreased creativity
- Risk of heart disease and stroke

- Impaired immune system
- Risk of Type 2 diabetes
- Decreased testosterone
- Increased stress
- Increased reaction time
- Aches
- Tremors
- Risk of obesity
- Irritability.

Excess cortisol also makes you look older because cortisol breaks down skin collagen, the protein that keeps skin elastic and smooth. In men, lack of sleep reduces testosterone levels and lowers sperm count.

The majority of people need seven to nine hours of sleep a night to feel rested. Very few people are at their best with less than seven hours, and few require more than nine. This is a serious problem since just over half the population gets less than the necessary seven hours of sleep each night, according to the National Sleep Foundation.

Story

We all have a different amount of sleep that we need in order to function at our maximum level. Scientists are discovering that our genes dictate this. The problem is that most people don't get enough sleep. Arianna Huffington was one of those frantic types of people who under-slept and over-worked until she collapsed unexpectedly from exhaustion one afternoon. Arianna Huffington is the chair, president and editor-in-chief of the Huffington Post Media Group, a nationally syndicated columnist and author of fourteen books.

In 2012, the site won a Pulitzer Prize for national reporting.

She has been named in Time Magazine's list of the world's 100 most influential people. She credits her success and well-being since then to the changes she's made to her sleep habits.

'I began getting 30 minutes more sleep a night until gradually I got to seven to eight hours. The result has been transformational,' Huffington says, adding that, 'all the science now demonstrates unequivocally that when we get enough sleep, everything is better. Our health, our mental capacity and clarity. Our joy at life, and our ability to live life without reacting to every bad thing that happens.'

"Finish each day before you begin the next, and interpose a solid wall of sleep between the two."

Ralph Waldo Emerson

A Technique to Help you Sleep Better

When I was younger, I found falling asleep and having a good deep sleep very difficult. My mind was racing with all the things that had happened during the day and, even worse, I would worry about all the things I had to do the following day and I would be wide awake for hours. I tried all sorts of things to fall asleep, and tried for force myself to sleep. This only made things worse as I would get angry, and my Inner Chimp would stay wide awake.

Things started to improve when I learned how to relax my whole body – starting with my feet and working slowly up – until I couldn't move any part of my body because I was so relaxed. But my mind was still wide-awake. Then I discovered a truth, which is that when we can't get to sleep it is because we are always thinking, and we are thinking in the future. Our thoughts are usually on things coming up such as meetings or presentations we have to organise, targets we are not meeting, financial worries, a relationship that isn't going well, maybe a health problem or... the list goes on.

Our job is to stop all that inner chatter. A technique I teach in my coaching sessions helps my clients in dramatic fashion. My suggestion to help with sleep is twofold.

Firstly, you have to challenge your belief system which tells you that you can never fall asleep quickly or that when you wake up you can't go back to sleep. This is dealt with in Chapter 11 on Belief Systems.

Secondly, you need to focus your thoughts on something in the past, which is a nice and happy memory. When you think forward to problems you may have, the mind explodes into multitudes of thought patterns searching for solutions to those problems. Your brain is simply doing what it was created to do: to solve problems and come up with solutions.

So when you get to bed and switch the light off, visualise a happy memory in detail as described in Chapter 13 on Visualisation and really re-live the memory. The mind is amazing and every detail of your past memory is stored there. All you have to do is access it. As you do this, you will remember more and more details.

At first you will find that you will only have a few moments in this memory before you find yourself back in your bed and wide awake. Don't worry about this – just say to yourself, 'where was I?' then go back to the memory. The more you practise this, the longer you will stay in the memory, and you will find yourself falling asleep. It's like riding a bike; you didn't just get on a bike and ride, it took practice. But once you learned, it became automatic – as will this sleep technique.

At this stage, your belief system is challenged and is changing. If you keep this going for a couple of weeks you will create a new belief system – a belief system that expects you to go to this memory and then fall asleep. Soon, your belief system will be so strong that you won't need to go to the memory; you will simply hit the pillow and within a few minutes be asleep.

My belief system is very strong in this area and I don't need to go to my memory anymore; I simply get into bed and know that I will be asleep in minutes. I tell myself that I will deal with anything important or stressful when I wake up at the set time, and meanwhile I will enjoy a long, restful and refreshing sleep.

Because of my strong belief system I subconsciously file away any negative thoughts and situations until I wake up at the allotted time. Thinking about these through the night won't help and will contribute to the chance of being affected by a multitude of potential health problems.

"Change your thoughts and you change your world."

Norman Vincent Peale

There are things that you can put in place to help you get a good night's sleep and the following 13 suggestions should help you achieve the important goal of a good night's sleep.

1. **Avoid caffeine drinks after lunch**
   Caffeine is a powerful stimulant that interferes with sleep by increasing the production of adrenaline and blocking sleep-inducing chemicals in the brain. Caffeine has a six-hour half-life, which means it takes a full 24 hours to work its way out of your system.

   When you do finally fall asleep, caffeine disrupts the

quality of your sleep by reducing rapid eye movement (REM) sleep, which is the deep sleep needed for your body to recuperate most. You'll wake tired, want to grab a cup of coffee or an energy drink to try to make yourself feel more alert, which very quickly creates a vicious cycle.

2. **Avoid communication devices at night**

   Short-wave blue light can increase your energy levels by halting the sleep-inducing hormone melatonin. The sun contains a lot of blue light in the morning then reduces it during the afternoon, so the body can start to produce melatonin.

   In the evening, the body isn't expecting any blue light. However, nowadays this comes in the form of laptops, iPads and mobile phones. This exposure impairs melatonin production and affects your ability to fall asleep, as well as the quality of your sleep. So it is best to avoid these in the evening – TV in most cases is fine as long as you sit far enough away.

3. **Don't use any medication**

   It's important to avoid any sort of sedative to help you sleep such as sleeping pills, alcohol or valium, as these disrupt your brain's natural sleep process. As you sleep your brain removes harmful toxins and it cycles through a series of stages, going through the day's memories and storing or discarding them, which causes dreams. Sedation of any sort interferes with this process, altering the brain's natural cycle.

4. **Develop a sleep routine**

   As you near your bedtime, start to slow everything down as if you are already starting to go to sleep. This means slowing your movements down and not having any stimulating things on the television that might 'wake you up'. Try to have the same routine every night, switching lights off and clearing things up as you go. Walk slowly and feel yourself getting sleepy as you get to your bedroom. Get ready for bed in a quiet, methodical way by setting your alarm and brushing your teeth, all with a relaxed feeling. As you get into bed and your head hits the pillow, use this final action as an anchor to fall asleep.

5. **Don't work in the evening**
   If you work in the evening, it puts you in an alert state when you should be switching off and winding down in readiness for sleep. Research shows that roughly 50% of people check their smartphones right until they go to sleep. Build in a system where you determine a time in the early evening where you will not check any devices until the morning. Put this in place and experience the benefits.

6. **Stop thinking**
   This sounds easier than it is, because it is impossible for the mind to actually switch off. Our inner voice or self-talk never ceases and is a constant dialogue. We may not be aware of it during the busy day, but once we lie down to go to sleep, we notice that we are thinking or talking to ourselves non-stop.

   Our minds can keep us awake with thoughts about what we need to do the following day or things that are troubling us. By paying attention to this, our brain does what it is created to do and that is to solve our problems, so it wakes up and gets going. After a few seconds, we are wide-awake and can't settle down to sleep. Our job is to switch the mind to something far more relaxing, and that is dealt with at the end of this chapter.

7. **Wake up at the same time every day**
   If possible, waking up at the same time each day helps the body move through the sleep cycle in preparation for

you to feel rested and alert at wake up time. Waking up at the same time every day improves your mood and sleep quality by regulating your circadian rhythm.

When you have a consistent wake-up time, your brain acclimates to this and moves through the sleep cycle in preparation for you to feel rested and alert at your wake-up time. Roughly an hour before you wake, hormone levels increase gradually (along with your body temperature and blood pressure), causing you to become more alert. This is why you'll often find yourself waking up right before your alarm goes off.

8. Reduce interruptions

Wherever possible, do your best to reduce interruptions that are under your control. If you have noisy neighbours, wear earplugs. Switch off the phone or any other device where someone can contact you when you should be sleeping. Don't drink too much at night to avoid going to the toilet. If the light comes in through your bedroom window, especially during the summer months, consider getting black out curtains.

9. Take sleep seriously

A fact of life is that when we prioritise something to a high level of importance we generally get it done. The same goes for sleep. Some people don't understand the importance and health benefits of sleep and so don't spend time developing the things which help them get a good night's sleep.

My job in this chapter is to get you to understand the importance of sleep. If you don't get to sleep within a few minutes and sleep soundly all night, then you need to take some action to improve the situation. I have developed a system that allows me to fall asleep within two to three minutes every night - and if I do wake up for any reason,

I will fall asleep again within a few minutes. This is down to my belief system and the techniques described in this chapter.

10. Learn to switch off

Meditation or Mindfulness improves the quality of sleep even if you can't increase the number of hours you sleep. At the Stanford Medical Centre, insomniacs participated in a six-week mindfulness meditation and cognitive-behavioural therapy course. At the end of the study, participants' average time to fall asleep was cut in half (from 40 to 20 minutes), and 60% of subjects no longer qualified as insomniacs. The techniques for this are covered in Chapter 16 on Mindfulness.

11. Breathe deeply

Deep breathing helps reduce your blood pressure and heart rate, releases endorphins and relaxes your body, priming you for sleep. Inhale for five seconds, pause for three then exhale for five seconds. Start with 10 repetitions and increase to 20. You should inhale using your belly not using your chest. See if you can learn to breathe using only your stomach and not your chest. If you do this correctly, your belly will rise and fall and your chest will stay in the same position. This method of breathing is used in meditation.

12. Write it down

Have a pad and pen next to your bed, and before you go to sleep write down anything on your mind. Then tell yourself that you will deal with all those things when you wake up and not think about then when you are in bed.

13. Don't read in bed

Your bedroom is for sleeping and I would advise you not to read in bed before going to sleep. My wife used to have trouble getting to sleep and she always read a book in bed before she went to sleep.

She found that she couldn't read a book during the day without feeling sleepy as she had established an anchor between reading and sleep and this annoyed her. So she decided to change her pre-sleep routine. The final hour before going to bed she now switches the TV off and gets a hot milky drink, then reads for a while. She then goes upstairs, brushes her teeth, gets ready for bed, puts the light out and falls asleep quickly. This routine is her new sleep system which works and allows her to read during the day now, whenever she wants, without feeling sleepy. She has established a new belief system.

Summary

- Sleep is far more important than many people realise.
- Lack of sleep can have serious health consequences.
- When you sleep, your brain removes toxic proteins from its neurons.
- Your body overproduces the stress hormone cortisol when it is sleep deprived.
- Most people need seven to nine hours of sleep a night to feel rested.
- There are various techniques available to help you sleep better.
- Learn to stop your inner chatter and relax.
- Challenge your belief system that tells you that you can never fall asleep quickly or that you can't go back to sleep if you wake up.
- Focus your thoughts on a pleasant memory from the past.
- Use the practical suggestions to help you get a good night's sleep.

"A ruffled mind makes a restless pillow."

Charlotte Brontë

Action Plan

1. Your job is to find a memory you have in the past which is pleasant and enjoyable. It helps if it is a memory that is quite relaxing and fun. Good examples would be a great holiday, a lovely Christmas day, a beautiful wedding, a fabulous meal out or a special day out.
2. Once you have come up with a memory with which you associate good feelings, you then need to visualise this memory in detail. When you have relaxed your body, go to this memory and remember the details of it. All the details are stored in your memory, and it's just a case of bringing them back. You will jump about from scene to scene, but that's okay as the picture starts to build and those nice feelings start to come back.
3. As you visualise, you will experience the feelings you felt on that day. You will feel good and the more you visualise, the more you will start to relax. To start with you will find yourself jumping back to your problems, and when this happens just say to yourself, 'Where was I?' and then go back there. After a few days, you will find this jumping happens less and less and you will become more involved in the memory and you will start to drift off to sleep faster.
4. If you wake up in the night to go to the toilet, keep the light off and try to stay in a semi-sleep state. Make sure you don't start to wake yourself up and believe that you will go back to sleep quickly when you get back into bed.
5. If you wake up, believe that you will fall asleep quickly. You have to develop your belief system so that it becomes real to you. Perception is reality and if you believe something, it becomes your reality.
6. Persevere with this and within a few days you will be sleeping better. Within a couple of weeks, you will be sleeping soundly. You will have a new belief system

in place that tells you that you can go straight to sleep when you go to bed, and that if you wake up for whatever reason you will go straight back to sleep within minutes.

7. When I go to bed using these techniques I fall asleep within three minutes, and if I wake up I fall back to sleep in about the same time. This is a combination of the techniques described and my very strong belief system.

Final Thoughts

Getting enough sleep is very important not only for our health and our ability to think clearly, but it also affects our looks. Not everyone can get to sleep easily in order to achieve their optimal functioning, but there are practical techniques that have been shown to help.

By practising these until they become ingrained and part of our belief system, the duration and quality of our sleep will be significantly improved. The resulting beneficial effects are well worth the effort involved – improved and adequate sleep patterns can be life-changing.

"There is a time for many words,
and there is also a time for sleep."

Homer, The Odyssey

Summary

Chapter 19

Summary

The information and techniques I have shared with you in this book are truly life-changing. If you decide to keep an open mind and try them out, you will be surprised at how quickly you can positively change the way you think, speak and act.

The Law of Attraction states that the emotions you send out on a daily basis come back to you in direct proportion. Your job is to be positive more than 50% of your day and to aim for a much higher percentage. On average I am at least 90% positive and, because of that, good things keep happening to me.

I use the various techniques in this book to reframe my negative thoughts and emotions into positive ones, so not only do I have a positive day but I create the situation to have a positive tomorrow. It seems too good to be true, but if you are happy and contented this will bring you more of the same the following day, week and month.

If you work through this book and apply the actions recommended, you will be surprised how quickly your thinking process changes for the better and how much pressure you can take without cracking under the strain.

You will learn to stay energised through healthy eating habits, and you will sleep better if you are struggling at the moment. You will have the tools to relax and to be 'in the present' more often, where you can 'just be' to recharge your batteries and rest your mind. You will have the tools to reframe from negative to positive very quickly and you will be more grateful for all the things in your life.

The Inner Chimp in your mind will be managed better and you will create a better 'belief system' to help you achieve more. You will learn how to benefit from the principles of the Law of Attraction and how to keep a positive mindset. You will create your own Dream Board, which will increase the chances of bringing the things you really want into your life.

There are no shortcuts to hard work and applying these techniques takes time and effort, but the results obtained are amazing. As you apply the five key pillars of Mental Resilience – Commitment, Motivation, Control, Self-Belief and Focus – to your life, you will see it improve in so many ways.

I challenge you to apply these principles to your life and let me know what improvements you see happening in a relatively short period of time. I am 61 years of age and I am just taking off on an exciting 19 year journey that will have many highs and some lows. But using everything described in this book, the lows will be tackled and overcome and the highs will be enjoyed.

Our best learning comes from mistakes we make and the problems we face so embrace these as you move on in life. Know that each problem or mistake we face teaches us something we need to learn, so we win when we are doing well and we win when we are facing problems.

About the Author

John Dabrowski is the founder of JD Mindcoach Ltd, a company that helps individuals and organisations develop world class Mental Resilience. John has experienced great challenges and adventures in his life, from being the last pick 'off the wall' at school, to playing basketball for England in the Commonwealth games.

He played basketball from the age of 12 and quickly improved by using the techniques of Mental Resilience that he discovered and developed. This led him into a professional basketball career where he played all over Europe, culminating in winning the Play-Off finals at Wembley live on BBC TV. In his latter playing days, he scored a British record of 98 points in a single match, which he credits to 'being in the zone.'

Following a serious back injury, he finished playing after the Play-Off victory and took up a position of Commercial Manager at Sunderland basketball club. It was here that he discovered a hidden talent for sales and marketing. He then became General Manager of the Manchester Giants basketball club, where with hard work and good management they were voted the best-promoted club in England by the English Basketball Association.

John then left the basketball world to enter the sales arena, initially in the capacity of regional sales executive for the Metro Radio station in Newcastle. He quickly established himself in the role and was soon promoted to regional sales manager where he flourished. He brought in record sales for the station, as well as hitting a record 19 monthly sales targets in a row.

Over the next 20 years, he worked for some outstanding design and advertising agencies where he learned excellent sales and marketing techniques. He reached director level and won various national accounts as well as looking after large key accounts. He learned great rapport-building techniques which helped him build his client base.

A few years ago, before he set up JD Mindcoach Ltd, he qualified as an NLP (Neuro Linguistic Programming) practitioner and coach, and completed various courses in Human Relations and Guided Imagery. He has attended many courses to develop his skills and is a member of the Professional Speaking Association.

John now runs Mental Resilience and Sales courses around the country to various sized organisations, including the Probation Trust, NatWest Bank, Kenwood, Salvation Army Housing, NHS, the Academy for Chief Executives, Nottingham University, Wakefield Housing and Hatstand Financial, to name a few. He has also run workshops in Gibraltar and Scotland, where they have been equally well-received. He has worked with hundreds of Chief Executives and Directors, inspiring them to achieve more.

He coaches executive clients from all corners of the country including the Isle of Man. He works individually to help them overcome challenges and develop new techniques to inspire them to achieve peak performance.

John's thriving speaking career includes the Rotary Club Convention, where he will be inspiring 650 delegates with his stories and humour. He is a regular on BBC Radio and has been interviewed on TV. He speaks at various events inspiring people with his stories and techniques. He has developed his speaking skills over the past few years and has a dream to speak all over the world.

He is an advocate of the Law of Attraction, which states that doing the right things and working hard brings amazing benefits to your life. John has used a raft of Mental Resilience techniques to help him succeed in life and to build his current successful business. He now shares these with people to help them discover things within that they weren't aware of, and to reach heights they never dreamed of.

John is 61 years of age with a plan to be speaking on stage at the age of 80 – he believes that when you boil life down to a core statement the following phrase he uses sums it all up:

"It's not how you start in life that counts, but how you finish!"

CONNECT WITH JOHN ON –

Linkedin – linkedin.com/in/johndabrowski
Twitter – @jdmindcoach
Facebook – facebook.com/jdmindcoach
Website – www.jdmindcoach.co.uk
AND ...
Email – john@jdmindcoach.co.uk

Mental Resilience Workshops

John's unique Mental Resilience Workshops are having a big impact on the people attending. They are fun and interactive with great take away value. The life-transforming techniques are beneficial to both business and personal life. The new positive mindset developed creates a new energy, resulting in much improved performance.

There are both half-day and full-day courses available. These include the Platinum Programme of six different workshops over six months, which take the attendees on a journey of self-discovery. The result of going through this programme is the ability to handle greater pressure, feel much more positive, and achieve a great deal more.

There are a series of other workshops available including advanced sales, communication, human relations, time management, body language and stress management.

Testimonials

"We wholeheartedly commend John's work to you. He delivers an impressive workshop, with an excellent range of practical Mental Resilience techniques to help individuals cope better when they are under stress and thrive whilst under pressure during the current challenging times."

Jane Geraghty, Chief Executive Officer Nottinghamshire Probation Trust

"John is a fabulous presenter. Great information shared. I will be using this at work and in my day-to-day life. The session was fun and interactive. I loved the clips and the involvement with the basketball. Very good and useful session. I have gone away feeling confident, motivated and ready to set goals. Thank you."

Louise Davis, Leaseplan UK

Public Speaking

John has a truly unique style of presentation, which is inspiring thousands of people across the country. He has been described as authentic, honest, gifted, and totally inspirational. He has spoken to audiences across the country with consistently positive feedback. He uses his basketball sporting background to great effect when illustrating business situations.

One of the things that really inspires people is that John is a living example of the content he delivers in his talks. He is 61 years of age and has a 19-year plan to be speaking on stage at the age of 80 – few people doubt this will happen!

During his life, he has faced many challenges: being the last off the wall in PE, not being able to speak English at the age of five, and not having the confidence to introduce a Professor to four students. Yet he has overcome all of these with techniques he shares in his talks.

Testimonials

"I was immediately blown away by John's engaging and honest style. As a business person, I regularly attend inspirational and motivational seminars. However, John's ability to fuse the dynamic demands of high-performance sports and the continuous challenges of modern business life

together in one seamless, simple and solutions focused way, was truly fantastic!"

Tony Ward, MD, Force 10 Recruitment

"Inspiring, energetic and engaging. These are the keywords I would use to describe what I saw today. John Dabrowski delivered a powerful talk that really captured not only my attention but his whole audience's. Sharing real life experiences that relate to and explore the wonderful world of the human mind, John has a natural charismatic flair that brings a fantastic energy to the room."

Ian Morris, EH Solicitors

Executive Coaching

The vast experience John has in the business and sporting world gives him a unique coaching style, which is appreciated by his wide range of executive clients. He uses various NLP techniques as well as good old-fashioned listening skills to help his client 'see the wood for the trees.'

There is something unique about a totally confidential coaching session where absolutely nothing is shared with anyone apart from John and his client. This gives the safe environment for total honesty and openness, which brings about amazing solutions to challenges faced by the clients.

The sessions are fun and interactive, and result in the client taking action plans forward together with great levels of accountability to get things done.